Mindful
Eating

Mindful Eating

Nourish your body and soul with
mindful meditations and recipes
using natural ingredients

Rachel Bartholomew and Mandy Pearson

CICO BOOKS
LONDON NEW YORK

For our families

This second edition published in 2017 by CICO Books
An imprint of Ryland Peters & Small Ltd
20–21 Jockey's Fields   341 E 116th St
London WC1R 4BW   New York, NY 10029

www.rylandpeters.com

First published in 2014

10 9 8 7 6 5 4 3 2 1

A CIP catalog record for this book is available from the Library of
Congress and the British Library.

ISBN: 978 1 78249 452 2

Printed in China

Editor: Elanor Clarke
Designer: Louise Leffler
Illustrator: Amy Louise Evans

Neither the authors nor the publisher can be held responsible for any
claim arising out of the use or misuse of suggestions made in this book.
If you are in any doubt about your health, please consult your doctor
before making any changes to your usual dietary and well-being regime.

Contents

Introduction

You Instinctively Know What Works

With so many different "diet" books on the market, you would be forgiven for wondering whether there's room to squeeze in yet another new approach to the way we involve food in our lives. We are bombarded with more books and advice about food and healthy-eating plans than ever before, yet people are still confused and end up doing nothing at all about the way they eat because they are simply unable to see what needs changing amid all the confusion. For others, this glut of information can lead to an unhealthy obsession with "healthy eating" (which now has its own medical term, "orthorexia"), religiously following the latest diet craze.

You will be relieved to know that this book is less about presenting a "new approach," and more about helping you find a way of **getting back to what we instinctively know works best** as far as food and eating are concerned. This isn't a "diet" book as such. We aim to show you how to listen and respond to your body's unique needs so that you can **fall in love with real food**, which will **nourish your health, well-being, and vitality.**

FOOD FOR THOUGHT

What does your instinct tell you about food?

Perhaps your instinct tells you that:

Real food is better than artifically enhanced "food products."

Slow food is more beneficial than fast food.

A balanced, varied diet and a positive attitude towards food simply cannot be improved.

Your instinct will often point you in the right direction if you slow down and make space to connect to this inner wisdom. Many people have lost their way when it comes to food, not only with the types and amounts consumed, but also with how it is involved in their lives.

Have you stopped listening to your instinct about food? Life is often too busy for this instinct to be heard. Now might be the time to start to tune into your instinct again.

Mindful eating helps you to fall in love with real food, which nourishes your health, vitality, and well-being.

Getting the Most out of Mindful Eating

Treat mindful eating as a journey. **View it as an exciting project** and **start to work through it step by step**, just as you would any other projects that you've been involved in, like re-designing a room or planning a menu for a special meal. You will notice simple exercises throughout this book, as well as recipes and guided meditations. We recommend that you immerse yourself in the complete process; **work through all the exercises and try out the recipes. Work with it** and it will work for you. We want to engage both your conscious and unconscious minds in the process of learning to eat mindfully. The conscious mind learns through logical explanation and the main body of each chapter will give it plenty to think about. The unconscious mind learns through imagery and symbolism and it will be reached by each chapter's opening story and meditation. An important first step is to **buy a beautiful book to use as a journal**, and perhaps also some lovely colored pens and pencils so that you can get involved in charting your progress and **writing down all the insights** that occur to you along the way.

"Never lose an opportunity of urging a practical beginning, however small, for it is wonderful how often in such matters the mustard-seed germinates and roots itself."

Florence Nightingale

Chapter 1

Mindfulness

The Touchstone

The Royal Library of Alexandria was said to house all the secrets of the ancient world. When it burned down, some time around 30BCE, only a few of the millions of scrolls that were housed there survived. One scroll in particular, which didn't look like much superficially, was sold to an old man for a small amount of money. When he examined the document closely he found an inscription that right at the bottom of the scroll. Written in golden letters, this inscription was perhaps the most valuable secret the world has ever known, "The secret of the touchstone." The man knew of the legend of the touchstone— it gave the person who discovered it the secret of eternal life. The scroll contained an ancient map showing the exact location of the salt-water lake containing the touchstone, along with many millions of other stones that looked just the same. This particular stone would feel warm and alive when you held it; the old man vowed to devote his life to finding it. He sold everything he owned and left for the lake. He found the spot, made camp, and set out to look for the touchstone. He picked up each stone, holding it to feel its temperature, and then dropped it back into the water. He continued for years, without ever finding the one. After ten years he finally picked up a stone that felt warm and alive. He held it in his hand for a moment and mindlessly, with a well-practiced throw, dropped the pebble back into the water with all the others.

What is Mindfulness?

Have you ever wondered how much of life you might be missing by operating on automatic pilot? People tend to miss the present moment because they are thinking about the past or worrying about the future.

Have you ever driven somewhere and arrived wondering how you got there? This is the kind of everyday mindlessness that most people experience all the time. It's easy to miss the journey when you are caught up in your own thoughts. It is also easy to get distracted from the job you're doing because in busy twenty-first century life there are always other demands on your attention. You might start to make a cup of coffee, then notice that a plant needs watering, let the dog out, and bring the laundry in, and then remember the coffee an hour later when it's gone cold.

Mindlessness prevents you from being in the moment. When you are doing what you have always done, in a mindless way, you are not in full and conscious control of your own life.

The Buddha said, **"The secret of health for both mind and body is not to mourn the past, worry about the future, or anticipate troubles, but to live in the present moment wisely and earnestly."**

The practice of mindfulness is steeped in the Buddhist tradition's rich history, which is over 2,500 years old. Yet **this collection of simple principles can offer many benefits** when applied to modern lifestyles. Mindfulness simply encourages you **to be wide-awake in whatever you are doing, whenever you are doing it.**

Professor Mark Williams, who developed Mindfulness-Based Cognitive Therapy (MBCT) in 2001 said: "Mindfulness is a translation of a word that simply means awareness…[it] is about learning to **pay attention, in the present moment, and without judgment**. It's like training a muscle—training attention to be where you want it to be. This reduces our tendency to work on autopilot, allowing us to **choose how we respond and react.**"

Benefits of Mindfulness

Mindfulness puts you back in control and enables you to **live with purpose**. It can allow you to have more insight into your inner and outer worlds, as well as **improve your ability to focus and enjoy the now**. It has been well known for thousands of years that **mindfulness practices have a positive impact on your health and well-being**. A recent study concluded that over the last two decades, Mindfulness-Based Stress Reduction programs (MBSR) have been shown to have **a positive impact** on anxiety, stress, depression, and addictive behaviors, and also **have a beneficial effect** on diseases such as hypertension, heart disease, and chronic pain.

Mindfulness and Self-Realization

A spiritual life can be grounded and a grounded life can be spiritual. There are no activities that are more worthy of your full attention than others. Sages say that **there are many paths to self-realization/enlightenment/increased awareness**, or however you wish to describe this awakened state. It may come through practicing formal meditation over many years, but **it may also be achieved through the informal practice of mindfulness in everyday tasks**.

Mindfulness puts you back in control and enables you to live with purpose.

Simple Principles of Mindfulness

The practice of mindfulness can be broken down into several key principles:

✱ **Be in the moment.** Take time to smell the roses and allow yourself to **switch from doing to being.**

✱ **Live on purpose.** You cannot choose your circumstances, but you can always **choose your response.**

✱ Know that **you always have the choice to change.**

✱ **Trust in yourself** and in your innate ability to know and **do what is right for you**.

✱ **Connect to the wisdom of your body. You know best** what you need.

✱ **Cultivate awareness**—of your patterns and habits, of your emotions.

✱ **Develop curiosity not judgment**. Curiosity opens you to the possibility of change, judgment closes you down.

✱ **Take responsibility (think response-ability)**. Taking responsibility for your world gives you the ability to **choose how you respond.**

✱ **Keep a beginner's mind. Stay open and flexible to new learning**—what you think you know can get in the way of your ability to **see what is really there.**

✱ **Learn acceptance of what is**—don't just pretend it's not happening. Don't be Cleopatra—(a Queen of denial!)

* **Enjoy the now—pay attention to the present moment**, it is a gift and it's all you've got.

* **Focus on gratitude** for what you have now—the true path to happiness is about appreciating what you have.

Mindfulness and Eating

*"The blazing fire makes flames and brightness
out of everything thrown into it."*

Marcus Aurelius

You can apply the principles of mindfulness to your eating habits. When you apply these principles to your eating, it helps you to **sharpen your focus** and start to thoroughly **enjoy your food again.** It can also significantly improve your health, both now and in the long term.

We do not claim that eating is the only path to enlightenment, but if you **become more mindful in whatever you do** it will **enrich your life**. Changing the way you eat can change the way you live, and if you re-evaluate your food practices you will become more enlightened about your life.

By applying the principles of mindfulness to your eating, you can begin to **make the food choices you want** to make for all the right reasons. Mindful eating puts you **back in control of your eating habits**, so that you can look and feel the way you want. Many people decide to change their eating habits to improve their size and shape, but the benefits are commonly far more wide-ranging. What we have often noticed is that when you **take control of** one aspect of your life, such as **your eating**, it's like lighting a flame that sparks change in many other areas of your life as well. The fabulous news is that change is generative and contagious. Not only do the changes filter through into different areas of your own life, but they often positively affect the lives of others around you, too. We hear time and time again from people who have completed our program that the sparks have also reached their families, friends, and colleagues.

Comments from people who have attended our mindful eating course

"Mindful eating brought back my mojo. I have made great new friends and found the confidence to buy and wear 'the red dress.' My food repertoire has increased. I have more energy and am able to seize the day." *Sue, 48*

"Life is now so much better for my family and me. Using all the strategies and nutritional information I learned on the course, I was able to turn my life around. I have lost nearly three stones in weight and I feel fitter than ever. I can now run five kilometers in twenty-five minutes." *Mandy, 32*

"When I started the program, I hoped to learn more about nutrition and healthy eating, and to work out where I was going wrong. I achieved all of this and more. I came away with a healthier, more positive outlook on life. I realized that stress was playing a huge part in my life and I decided to make some major changes. I have now resigned from a full-time job and I am about to sign the lease on my long-held dream of a new artisan chocolate shop." *Jacqui, 45*

Our Mindful Eating Ethos

Years of experience working individually with clients who want to change their eating habits has taught us that it isn't enough to teach people what they need to do, it is also essential to support them with strategies to put this advice into practice. We have found that working together, **combining nutritional and psychological wisdom, has significant positive influence on long-term outcomes.**

For us, food is about so much more than simply the contents of a plate. The way you choose to involve it in your life and think about it is just as important, if not more so. We aim to provide you with a grounded, holistic approach to food and eating that will help you to:

✶ Become fascinated by your food;

✶ Understand what constitutes healthy food for you;

✶ Improve your relationship with food;

✶ Connect with your inner wisdom.

Apply mindfulness principles to eating and really start to enjoy food again.

Eating mindfully will help you to make permanent changes to your diet, lifestyle, and the way you think and feel.

You won't have to endure your food and feel deprived of your favorite treats. This is about **you taking responsibility for your own health** because you want to, and making healthy, tasty, nutritious food choices.

This is not about your diet consisting of 100% superfoods, but rather about **creating a healthy balance**, including all of those lovely foods and drinks, such as chocolate or wine, which you may have felt you had to give up completely to get where you want to be. The aim is to achieve a healthy balance that you're in control of and feel great about.

We want you to **embrace the whole idea of food** as something to **linger over and enjoy**, something to **share as a family** or with friends. Mindful eating is about enjoying preparing food, cooking, and being cooked for—when you do that you will **fall in love with food again.** It's about you, your health and happiness, and that of those around you. It's about you making the most of every single moment in your life.

"Be happy in the moment, that's enough. Each moment is all we need, not more."

Mother Teresa

FOOD FOR THOUGHT

Go for a mindful sensory walk. Observe everything you see, extend your vision to places you wouldn't usually notice. Many people look down and talk to themselves when they are walking, missing what's around them. Practice walking while looking up—look for squirrels and birds in the trees. Look to the right and left. Get a sense of what's in front of you and behind you. Notice what new sights you take in. Now shift your awareness to the sounds around you. Become attuned to any noise from the street, any bird or animal sounds, the rhythm of your feet on the ground. Listen to your breathing. Turn your attention to each compass direction and hear the sounds from different locations as you allow your hearing to become more and more acute. Now focus on your movement.

Move as slowly as you can, noticing each time your feet touch the ground. Be aware of what every part of your body does as it moves. Now move in a different way. You could spin around or safely walk backwards. You could walk on a wall like a child, or skip as fast as you can, just to revel in different kinds of movement. Connect to your inner emotions and check out how you feel.

MINDFUL INFUSIONS

Choose one of these fragrant herbal infusions or invent your own. We find that glass tea tumblers work really well, as you can fully appreciate not only the refreshing taste and aroma, but also the visual delights. You can sweeten any of the teas with a dash of manuka honey, simply adjust to your taste.

SIMPLE MINT TEA

———

2-3 sprigs of fresh mint

Freshly boiled water

Place the mint sprigs into your favorite tea tumbler.

Pour over hot water.

Leave to steep for a few minutes and you will notice the water start to turn slightly green.

Savor and enjoy.

Mindful tea notes: This simple, refreshing mint tea has long been used as a natural digestive aid.

It works well if sipped slowly after a meal.

ROSEMARY TEA

2-3 tsp finely chopped fresh rosemary leaves

Freshly boiled water

Add the fresh rosemary to your favorite tea tumbler.

Pour over the hot water and leave to steep for a few minutes.

Enjoy immediately or strain mixture first depending on your preference.

Mindful tea notes: Rosemary is associated with memory and is a lovely tea when you need focus and concentration on your side.

LEMON, GINGER, AND LEMONGRASS TEA

1 inch ginger, peeled and sliced into long thin strips

1 organic, unwaxed lemon

A few seeds from a cardamom pod

1 stalk lemongrass

Freshly boiled water

Press down on the ginger slices and cardamom seeds with the back of a teaspoon to release the flavors and place them in your favorite tea tumbler.

Slice the top and bottom off the lemongrass stalk and then slice in half lengthways, remove the outer layer, and place sliced inner sections into your tumbler.

Pour over hot water and leave to steep for a few minutes.

Squeeze the juice from the lemon and add to the tumbler.

Stir well and enjoy.

Mindful tea notes: The combination of lemon and ginger is energizing, while the extra cardamom adds spicy warmth to boost your metabolism. This is our favorite morning brew.

Chapter 2

Diet and Lifestyle

Acres of Diamonds

The year 1869 was a significant turning point in the history of South Africa—it was the year the Star of South Africa diamond (the rock upon which the economic success of South Africa was built) was discovered close to the banks of the Vaal River. Diamond fever quickly spread through the country and into the heart of one particular farmer living close to the discovery site. He was so taken by the possibility of great riches that he sold his farm and all his belongings and set out to search the continent for diamonds. The years passed and he worked tirelessly, but unfortunately he never found even the smallest chip.

Some time later, the new owner of the farm picked up an oddly shaped rock, about the size of a duck's egg. He liked the look of it so much that he put it on display on his mantelpiece. One day a visitor dropped in and, on seeing the rock, flew into a flurry of excitement. He told the farmer that it was the biggest diamond in the rough that he'd ever seen. "Really?" said the farmer, "my land is covered in them!"

The farm turned out to be the Kimberley Diamond Mine, one of the richest mines the world has ever known. The original farmer literally had been standing on "acres of diamonds" before he sold the farm in search of riches.

Western Diet and Lifestyle

Today, we rarely sit down and enjoy a relaxed meal. Eating on the run, at our desk, or in the car is now the norm. Everything about the average twenty-first-century Western lifestyle is fast, and that includes our approach to food. Unfortunately, we now know that the breakneck pace at which many rush through life is not only stressful, but is also causing major health problems. It has been estimated that around 75% of all visits to doctors are due to stress-related ailments and disorders. It is also a sad fact that the typical modern Western diet is not something to feel proud of. In fact, the words "Western diet" are now synonymous with negative health effects. For us, the term "Western diet" encompasses not just the types of food that are commonly consumed, but also the way in which they are eaten. A culture of fast food pervades throughout the Western world; fast-food restaurants are big business and if you don't have time to stop you can "drive through" to make it even quicker. Superstores have a "fast lane," you can buy "express coffee," and you can make a "meal in a minute" at the touch of a button.

Health Risks and the Western Diet

The typical Western diet is now strongly associated with an increase in obesity in general, and type 2 diabetes in particular. These negative health effects are being seen in young children—obesity is becoming one of the most common pediatric disorder in the developed world and approximately one third of children are either overweight or obese. Unfortunately, the longer-term impact of childhood obesity includes an increased risk of type 2 diabetes and cardiovascular health problems as an adult.

The fast-paced Western way of life and digestive disorders often go hand in hand. Eating on the run or in a stressful, hurried state can wreak havoc on your digestion, which in turn can have an impact on your overall health.

Health risks associated with the under-performing Western diet go even further, and we now know that dietary factors have a role to play in some cancers and many other chronic diseases.

The simple fact is that most people are already well aware that the typical Western diet and lifestyle don't bring out the best in us, or **support optimal health and well-being**. We also know that many people want to make changes but struggle to know what to do and how to put these changes into practice, surrounded by a sea of confusing and conflicting information. We know that there is a multitude of different "diets" and "diet foods" on offer, perhaps more than ever before, yet we are still set on the same course, sailing right into the eye of an obesity storm.

Your Health History

"If you do not change direction, you may end up where you are heading."

Lao Tzu

Your current health is a product not just of your own dietary choices but also of the choices of your parents, grandparents, and maybe even their ancestors too. **Your food choices might well have an impact** not just **on the health of your children**, but **on that of your grandchildren and perhaps even on the health of your grandchildren's offspring**. Now is the time to **bring the focus right back to good nutrition** and to make changes to benefit your own health and that of future generations.

The positive message sitting at the sometimes sharp, uncomfortable edge of all of this is that while food may well be working against many of us at the moment, **it is completely possible to shift your dietary patterns towards those that work for you again**. You can move toward ways of eating that promote optimal health and longevity, significantly reduce the risks of common chronic diseases, and that actively **seek to promote an overall sense of well-being**. You just need to decide to **take the first step in a new direction** and, if you take a look around, you will notice that others are starting to do the same.

Slow Food

In 1986, "Slow Food" emerged in Italy, an international movement founded by Carlo Petrini to resist the opening of a fast-food outlet on the Spanish Steps in Rome. Promoted as an alternative to fast food, with the ethos that "everyone has a right to good, clean, and fair food," the group now has over 100,000 members with branches in over 150 countries, and it's growing (fast!). The idea of fast food is anathema to the traditional Mediterranean way of life, where **every meal is a social, colorful, ceremonious feast** where local artisan food producers are celebrated, and where consumers can **be in touch with the origins** of their food. Even the process of choosing food at the local market is a **ritualistic and sociable event.** This is, we believe, what real food is about.

How have we arrived at this place where food choices and the way we involve food in our lives seem to be working against us, rather than with us?

A Very Short History of Diet

If you journey back to the beginning of humankind's relationship with food, you will find that hunting and gathering was a central part of life and that daily "work" focused on finding food and other elements essential for survival. The hunter-gatherer concept of sharing—that is, the giving of something without immediate expectation of return—was a core value for early tribes. The hunter-gatherer mentality was gradually replaced by agriculture and animal husbandry. The Industrial Revolution, which took place some 250 years ago, brought about further changes, which increased food production and processing. In more recent years, we have seen significant changes in the way food is produced, with widespread use of pesticides and fertilizers in farming, increased refining and processing of foodstuffs, and technological advances that have disrupted the natural food chain. Social attitudes toward food have also changed dramatically over the years. Many couples and families now struggle to find the time to share meals together. Precious communication around the table each day is sadly no longer the norm and the maxim that **"families that eat together, stay together"** has been forgotten. For most people, the deep-rooted connection to food with which we evolved has also disappeared.

There is some debate that these dietary and social changes have happened too quickly from an evolutionary perspective, leaving our bodies unable to adapt successfully, and so causing health problems. Perhaps it is time to question whether we really want to adapt to the diet and lifestyle changes that are happening around us and that mainly serve to disconnect us from real food and our original hunter-gatherer instincts.

For hunter-gatherers, **food represents much more than a collection of nutrients on a plate.** Food is sacred nourishment, and the act of eating nurtures a strong spiritual connection between those who share a meal. Hunter-gatherers **revere food and give thanks for every meal.**

Unlike the contemporary Western relationship with food, hunting and gathering is a way of life that has profound meaning for its practitioners. Hunter-gatherers have a strong and ever-present connection to the land, an unbreakable bond that gives this way of life such a strong sense of meaning. Perhaps it is time to reconnect with our hunter-gatherer roots.

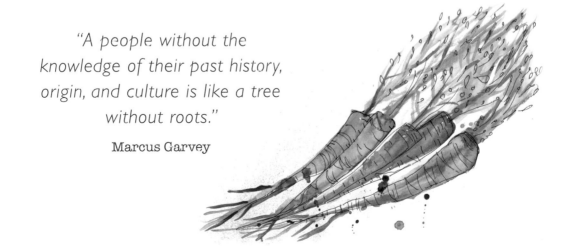

"A people without the knowledge of their past history, origin, and culture is like a tree without roots."

Marcus Garvey

FOOD FOR THOUGHT

The next time you sit down for a meal, take a moment to think about the different ingredients that have come together just to make this one dish. Now take this thought exercise one step further. How would you go about producing this meal and all its ingredients completely from scratch? What would that involve? Hunting? Farming? Growing? Processing? How long would it take? What space, equipment, and materials would you need? Would you need any help?

From this space you can start to acknowledge the collective effort that goes into your food and also start to nurture a connection to where your food has really come from (i.e. the soil not the supermarket). Finally, think about who and what you would give thanks to for each individual part of your meal.

Next time you tell yourself that you don't have time to sit down and eat, be it on your own or with others, think back to this exercise and about the collective time, effort, and wisdom that goes into your food.

CAMPFIRE FISH SERVED WITH HERB DRESSING AND SLOW-BAKED SWEET POTATO

Connect to your roots with this simple dish that gives campfire cooking a nutritious twist.

Serves 4

CAMPFIRE PAN-FRIED WHITE FISH AND BAKED SWEET POTATO

4 thick skinless white fish fillets

3 sweet potatoes

Olive oil

Salad leaves, such as rocket or watercress

Wrap the sweet potatoes in aluminium foil and place directly into the coals of your campfire. Remove after approximately an hour. Scrape the flesh out of the skins and mash together with some olive oil, sea salt, and black pepper.

Pour a dash of olive oil into a frying pan and place on a cooking grate over the campfire. Heat the oil and add the fish fillets. The heat will be less direct than on a hob so they will likely take longer to cook. Turn them over regularly. When the meat is a shiny, white color and readily flakes, your fish is ready to eat.

Serve on a bed of sweet potato mash, topped with herb dressing and accompanied by the fresh salad leaves.

HERB DRESSING

This tasty and nutritious dressing is best if it is prepared at home, before you go camping.

Handful of fresh flat-leaf parsley, stems discarded

2 large garlic cloves

6 tbsp olive oil, plus extra for greasing

1 tbsp fresh oregano

1 tsp ground cumin

Large pinch of dried chili flakes

Put the parsley, garlic, oil, oregano, cumin, and chili in a cup and blend with a stick blender until the herbs are finely chopped and combined

Finding a New Way Forward

It is tempting to look for a quick-fix solution to this long-standing problem, which we now know has taken many years to become fully ingrained in our lives. Just like a Band-Aid though, a quick fix doesn't usually last for long. You need to **get right to the root of the issue** so it can be dealt with at that level. **This is the most effective route to lasting change.**

We're not offering a quick fix and we don't have a magic wand either. What we are offering is a long-term solution to a long-standing problem. We want to help you to **find your way again with food** and **become much more mindful about your food choices** and the way you **involve food in your life.** We offer you the tools you'll need to put yourself in complete and conscious control of eating habits that will **nourish you from the inside out**, not just for a day, a week, or a few months, but for good. How does that sound to you?

Mindful eating can help you to:

✶   Nurture a healthy relationship with food;

✶   Understand which foods nurture you best;

✶   Re-establish a connection with real food;

✶   Learn how food can best serve you in a twenty-first-century setting.

What Kind of Eater Are You?

Busy eater: I tend to gulp down my food. I often rush my food or eat on the run. I do other things while I'm eating like text, tweet, read, or watch television. **Mindful eating will help you slow down and make time for your food.**

Fuel eater: I'm not really interested in food. I eat to live, I don't live to eat. I eat when it's convenient but I sometimes forget to eat, particularly if I'm stressed or ill. I see food as a bit of a chore. **Learn how to enjoy your food by eating mindfully.**

Convenience-food junkie: Takeout is my mainstay—I eat takeout in one form or another several times a week. **Apply the principles of mindful eating and you will soon value the whole process of creating a meal, from the production of the food and its preparation, through to savoring every mouthful.**

Reluctant chef: I'm not a good cook and I don't enjoy cooking. If others don't cook for me, I don't eat properly. **Discover how easy it is to make simple, delicious, and nutritious meals with mindful eating.**

Social eater: If there's only me, there's no point in cooking. I can't really be bothered to make an effort unless I am cooking for other people. **Eat mindfully and learn how to value yourself more so that you put just as much care and attention into your own meals as you do for those you prepare for others.**

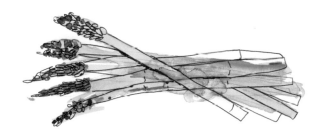

Fussy eater: There are only certain foods that I like. My food intake is limited to tried and tested favorites. **Mindful eating encourages you to do things differently. Every meal is an opportunity for a new start.**

Grazer: I don't eat proper meals but I do graze constantly—I keep going back to the cabinets for snacks and I tend to "taste" lots of food as I'm cooking it. **Use mindful eating to bring awareness to your habits and make conscious food choices.**

Problem eater: My life is a constant battle with food and I wish I could just give it up and not have to think about it again. **Learning how to eat mindfully will help you make friends with food again.**

Comfort eater: I eat when I'm unhappy. If I have a stressful conversation or a tough day at work, I find myself staring into the refrigerator for inspiration. **Using the principles of mindful eating, you can learn how to recognize when you are eating for reasons other than hunger.**

Habitual eater : I eat the same things at the same time on the same day every week, just like my parents and grandparents did before me. **Dare to try something different by eating mindfully.**

Yo-yo dieter: I have tried every diet, pill, and potion available in my attempts to lose weight, but I just can't keep off the weight. **Eat in a healthy, balanced way with mindful eating and achieve your healthy, ideal weight.**

The chef: I live to eat. My life revolves around food preparation and eating. I know I eat too much but I can't help it. **Mindful eating will teach you how to appreciate every mouthful and restore a healthy balance.**

Treat eater: Food is my favorite way to treat myself when I need a lift. Diets and healthy food are boring. **Learning to eat mindfully will help you to appreciate nutritious food as a treat.**

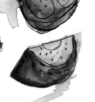

Calorie controller: I know the calorific content of every item of food I eat. I always choose low-calorie meals but I'm not happy with my body or my relationship with food. **Mindful eating will allow you to reconnect with real food again and leave the calorie counting behind.**

Learning to eat mindfully will help you **make gains in your health and fitness, get back in touch with your body's natural wisdom** about what it needs to thrive, **begin to glow from the inside out,** and transform your relationship with food so that you love what you eat and eat what you love.

In this book you will find out how to:

★ Gain confidence about what to eat and how;

★ Savor your food and make every mealtime a celebration;

★ Re-connect with the wisdom of your own body and listen to what you need;

★ Be happy about your health and fitness and your way of eating;

★ Make some permanent changes in your life that will benefit you for good;

★ Feel great about food from the inside out;

★ Fall in love with food again;

★ Nourish a spiritual connection with your food.

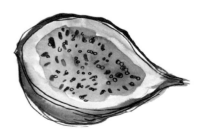

FOOD FOR THOUGHT

Make cooking a meditation. As you cook your favorite dish, remove any distractions and bring your awareness to the moment. First, become aware of your breathing and then gradually expand your awareness so that you are keenly aware of everything around you and within you. Slow down the process of assembling your ingredients, gathering each one at a time, and noticing their different qualities. Pick up a knife and feel it in your hand before you begin to chop the first ingredient; perhaps it is an onion. As you slice through its skin, become aware of its layers, texture, and color. Pay attention to the aroma, texture, shape, and color of each vegetable as you add it to the mix. Notice the temperature of the stovetop, the sounds as you chop; heighten your senses to be aware of each movement you make and be present as you stir the dish. Reflect on the concept that what you are doing is a metaphor for your whole life. You are assembling the ingredients for a happy, healthy life, adding revitalizing ideas and thoughts and mixing them together with some seasoning to spice up your day. Each offering you make and give to the world is unique and new. The finished dish is always something over and above the ingredients you started with, and you cannot always see what form the dish will take by simply examining the ingredients. There comes a point when you just need to leave all the ingredients simmering for a while. Do something else that you enjoy during this time while all the ingredients blend into something truly special. You need to give it time to cook; you won't improve the dish by continuously checking to see if it's ready. Give it the time it needs before you fully enjoy the end result of your work.

THREE SISTERS SOUP

Try this irresistible recipe for Three Sisters Soup. The "three sisters" of the title are the beans, corn, and squash that form an indelible part of native American-Indian cuisine.

¼ cup/50g dried butter beans

4 ripe Italian plum tomatoes (such as Roma)

1 large fresh jalapeño chili

4 garlic cloves, unpeeled

2 tbsp olive oil

1 onion, chopped

2 cobs/ears of fresh (sweet)corn, shucked

4oz/100g small yellow squash (pattypan or similar), quartered

4oz/100g fine green beans, trimmed and halved

2 cups/500ml vegetable stock

2 tbsp freshly squeezed lime juice

A handful of fresh cilantro/coriander sprigs, roughly chopped

Sea salt

Serves 4

Soak the butter beans in cold water overnight. Drain and put in a large saucepan with sufficient cold water to cover. Bring to the boil, reduce the heat and simmer, uncovered, for 1 hour or until tender. Drain and set aside.

Preheat the oven to 425°F (220°C) Gas 7. Put the tomatoes, chili, and garlic on a baking sheet and cook in the preheated oven for about 10–15 minutes until the skins darken and begin to blister. Remove the baking sheet from the oven, transfer everything to a clean plastic bag and seal. When cool enough to handle, peel the tomatoes, chili, and garlic. Discard the skins and coarsely chop the flesh. Set aside.

Heat the oil in a large saucepan set over medium heat. Add the onion and (sweet)corn with a pinch of salt and cook for 10 minutes, stirring often until softened. Stir in the tomato mixture, squash, green beans, butter beans, and stock, and bring to a boil. Reduce the heat to medium and simmer, uncovered, for 10 minutes until the green beans are tender. Stir in the lime juice, garnish with a few small sprigs of cilantro/coriander, and serve.

Chapter 3

Getting Started

Live On Purpose

There is a Sufi story about a tinsmith who was falsely accused of a serious crime and imprisoned for life in a high-security jail. As the days and months passed, he purposely built up a cordial relationship with his jailer. When the time was right he said: "I am a very religious man and it would be a great favor to me if you would allow me to have my own prayer mat from home." The jailer saw no reason not to do this, so by design the tinsmith's wife made him a very special mat and brought it in. A little later he engineered another conversation with his jailer. "I don't want to waste my life. I know your family is poor and I have great skill as a tinsmith, why not let me make myself useful to you by making some items from metal for you to sell at the soukh?" The jailer acquired tools for the tinsmith, who began to work away happily.

Several weeks later the jailer opened the cell door to find that the tinsmith was gone. Many rumors spread in the town about how this had happened. Some years later the tinsmith, in his absence, was cleared of the crime he was accused of when the real criminal confessed. The king put out an edict that, should the tinsmith return to tell his story, there would be no repercussions. The tinsmith returned and began to tell his story to the packed court. "It's a matter of living on purpose; you see, I had a plan. I made friends with the guard. I acquired the rug into which my wife (a weaver) had woven the design of the prison lock, which she had acquired from our friend the locksmith. I then came up with a way to get some tools and studied the design of the lock daily while I prayed so I could fashion the perfect key."

Finding Your "Why"

People have very different reasons for beginning a mindful eating program. It may be that you want to change the way you look, change your size and shape, or that you have had a health crisis that has made you **review your eating habits**. Perhaps you are thinking about the fitness benefits of eating in a mindful way. Maybe you want to change certain eating habits or your long-term patterns and inherited beliefs about food. It may even be that for you, food is a spiritual path to take you closer to self-realization. If you become mindful of your reasons for starting the program, chances are you will get to where you want to be and start to eat the way you want to eat.

The Importance of Setting a Direction

"Imagination is everything.
It is the preview of life's coming attractions"

Albert Einstein

Stephen Covey advises that we always **"begin with the end in mind."** Starting any endeavor without a clear objective is like expecting a GPS to get you to your destination without a ZIP code. If you don't know where you're going, you won't know when you get there. You're also likely to waste energy driving around. If you program the GPS with your intended destination, you **make sure you end up on the right road.**

If you have a clear idea about where you want to be, you **set a direction for your unconscious mind.** Incredible things can be achieved with focused intention. Scientists have even identified specific parts of the brain that help make this happen, such as the reticular activating system (RAS), which works with your visual cortex to **call your conscious attention to things that are important** to you in reaching your goals. Have you ever thought about buying a specific brand of car and noticed that once you start looking, you see it everywhere? It's the same when you learn about a new subject—you suddenly hear about it all the time because you are alert to that information.

The RAS acts as a tracking device that directs you to things that are important to you and filters out everything else. If you **become really clear about what you want**, your unconscious mind will constantly search for ways to help you achieve it.

If you **trust your mind** to do this for you, you can let go of the need to know the details of how **you'll get to your goal.** All you need to do is make some time every day to dream and set up mindful intentions for whatever you desire. At some point in your past, you may have been told you shouldn't daydream, yet this is the best way to access your unconscious resources. Nothing can happen unless you can conceive of it in your mind first. Moments of insight and creative solutions to problems come when you **allow your conscious focus to relax** and drift into a slower brain-wave state. Steven Spielberg has said, "I don't dream at night, I dream all day; I dream for a living." We want to teach you to dream mindfully in a way that helps you get where you want to be.

The Conscious and the Unconscious Mind

We often talk about being in two minds, but did you know that you actually do have two minds? Each of us has both a conscious and an unconscious mind. Your conscious mind is responsible for your **focus in this moment** and shifts from thought to thought like a torch beam moving from one place to another. For example, you may be thinking about the previous sentence or about what you're having for dinner, then looking at the time, planning tomorrow, or remembering last night. This is the conscious mind in action and it can only focus on seven to nine things at any given time.

There is, however, so much more going on below the surface. Your unconscious mind takes in the whole picture like a floodlight. It can process up to three million pieces of information per second. For example, your unconscious mind will now be registering information you are not aware of like the color of the walls, the sounds from outside, and the texture of your chair.

Freud used an iceberg as a representation of awareness, with the conscious mind being the tip of the iceberg and the unconscious mind the huge mass below the surface.

You could also think of it as a rider and a horse. The conscious mind, like the rider, can decide where to go, then guide and encourage the horse. The unconscious mind, like the horse, is completely neutral and impartial—it will carry out the instructions you give it, so you need to **be clear, positive, and assertive.** If you don't know the direction you want to go, you won't get anywhere. If the horse doesn't trust the rider, you also won't get anywhere. It's important to take good care of the horse, feed it well, and build a good relationship to **get the best performance** from it. It is counterproductive to micromanage how the horse gets you there—analyzing every step it takes will not help.

Learn to dream mindfully in a way that helps you get where you want to be

FOOD FOR THOUGHT

Look at the bigger picture

Sit down and allow your chair to support you as much as it can. Find a point on the wall in front of you and slightly above eye level. As you gently focus on that point, you may start to notice that everything around it starts to become a little hazy as your awareness becomes completely focused. This is how you are when you're working consciously on a specific task, pouring all your energy into one place such as reading a book or watching television: the conscious mind is fully occupied with one task. It's always good to remember that there is also a wider perspective, another way of looking at things. So, as you keep your eyes on that same point, begin to widen your vision to take in the view to either side of it. Keep broadening your perspective to include what you can see in a wider and wider arc, in your peripheral vision, until you can almost imagine that your field of vision extends to the far corners of the room. As you continue to broaden your horizon you may notice that you can be aware of so much more that is going on beside you and behind you than you had noticed previously.

Opening up to the big picture is a great way of learning new things, and you may be aware of just how calm you feel because it is impossible to feel stressed while you're in this relaxed state. You can come out of this state as soon as you wish, because you will have lots of opportunities to practice accessing your unconscious mind in this way as you learn how to be mindful.

Living on Purpose

Aldous Huxley told us to "dream in a pragmatic way." We've all set goals in the past that end up being quickly abandoned, especially at New Year. For a goal to be truly motivating, it has to appeal to both your unconscious and conscious minds.

There are two key principles that will help you create a compelling vision for your healthy future:

1) YOU'LL NEVER HIT A TARGET YOU CAN'T SEE

Your unconscious mind is highly responsive to images. Your mind generates feelings based on images, and feelings are the fuel that drives you. The way you respond to "reality" is determined by how you present things to yourself in your mind and not by what's "really there." Two people looking at a piece of broccoli on their plate can respond in different ways according to how they represent "broccoli" to themselves. If one had been force-fed veggies as a child, for example, they would see the broccoli differently from someone who immediately calls to mind past experiences of enjoying it and imagines its health benefits.

When you know this, you can **start to take control** of what you're picturing in your mind in order to have different, better responses.

Just as a beautifully laid table with white napkins, candles, and delicate crystal will make a meal more appealing, the images of your goals, which you create in your mind, will make them either more or less compelling to you. Successful sportspeople know that visualization improves performance; practicing shooting basketball hoops or kicking the ball into the net in your imagination will enhance your ability to do it for real. The brain does not distinguish between imagination and memory, so each time you **visualize a goal,** you give yourself an experience of achieving it, which creates a memory of having done it. You are creating new neural pathways to success.

2) MAKE IT ALL ABOUT YOU

Picture a large bus in your mind.

Look through the window and see yourself sitting on one of the seats.

Where do you choose to sit?

People answer this question in many different ways and there's no right or wrong answer. We've noticed, however, that people rarely choose to put themselves in the driving seat. This is exactly how many of us operate on a daily basis, allowing ourselves to be swept along by the tide of events, which happens throughout our lives. While it's true that you can't always control what happens around you, it's also true that you can **be in control of your own life** or, in other words, be mindfully in charge of your own bus.

Goals that are truly achievable are those over which you have control. If you make your goals dependent on other people, "I want my whole family to start eating mindfully with me," or dependent on external circumstances, "I will win the lottery," you are putting yourself in the passenger seat. Make your goals about you. See yourself introducing mindful eating into your daily life, sharing it with your family, and feeling good about it. See yourself living the life of your dreams. Set up images and feelings in which **you have all the support and resources you need** and then stop worrying about how that will happen.

Don't Pay Attention to This Next Bit

People spend a lot of time daydreaming about what they don't want rather than what they do want. This is called worrying. Interestingly, the root of the word 'worry' comes from the old English word "wyrgen," which means to strangle. Worrying can seriously damage your ability to get where you want to go. Every time you talk or think about what you don't want or what you want to avoid you will make big bright pictures of it. The common example is "don't think of a pink elephant." No, really, stop it! You cannot *not* think about it until you've thought about it first. What you focus on is what you get. The whole concept of "losing weight" or "giving up" something focuses on the negative. This is often why, when people are on a diet, they are constantly thinking about food, which is no wonder, because they are constantly making bright mental pictures of the foods they don't want to or are unable to eat. "I can't eat cake." "I shouldn't eat chocolate." "Whatever I do, I can't think about a big gooey chocolate cake calling to me from the kitchen." What you focus on expands, so choose your focus wisely.

FOOD FOR THOUGHT

Keep your eye on the prize

Whenever an issue comes up for you, instead of worrying about it, get into the habit of immediately refocusing mindfully on what you do want. Use the time you would have spent worrying to envisage the best-case scenario/end result that you do want. If you are in a traffic jam, instead of giving yourself a hard time worrying that you're going to be late, shift your thinking to what you do want. Picture the traffic beginning to move. See yourself arriving on time and use the extra time you have to do something more productive, such as meditate or plan.

Next time you are tempted by less healthy food, instead of telling yourself "I can't eat the cake, I don't want to be overweight, I don't want to eat mindlessly," start making bright pictures of yourself as you make a better food choice. See yourself taking the time to eat well. See the long-term consequences of doing this. Picture yourself glowing with well-being and loving healthy food. If your goal is to sit down and enjoy every meal, instead of telling yourself "I must not eat on the run" and worrying about that, picture yourself making the time you need to eat mindfully. Make up compelling images of the benefits you will get from doing this and think about how great it will feel when you reach your goal.

Another unwanted consequence of focusing on what you don't want is the impact this has on your motivation over time. Thinking about what you don't want, that is the negative consequences of your current behavior, can be highly motivating in the short term because pain is certainly a powerful, immediate motivational force, but this effect will fade over time and leave you feeling negative about your goals. You may even feel that you will be unable to obtain them.

Think about it this way. Would you walk across a foot-wide plank, 30-feet long, suspended between two building, 200 feet above street level? Probably not. Now ask yourself, would you do it if the building you were in was on fire and you needed to get out immediately? Probably yes.

For some people this is the only way they know how to motivate themselves. They only get fired up to lose a few pounds when their summer vacation is a month away because they don't want to look bad in a bathing suit, or they re-evaluate their eating habits only when they have a health scare. This is known as "away from" motivation. They want to get away from pain. The trouble is that although this works effectively in the short term, as soon as the crisis is over, motivation drops, so when you are no longer in the danger zone (health scare or impending holiday) motivation plummets and you go back to the same old habits until crisis strikes again. This leads to the classic yo-yo cycle.

If, on the other hand, you **motivate yourself towards positive long-term goals**, you will sustain your motivation over time and, what's even better, the closer you get to your goal, the more motivated you will be. This will only happen, however, if you **create goals that are** equally as **compelling** as the "away from" goals would be. So, for example, you may not walk across that foot-wide plank for $20 but would you walk across the plank if you knew that doing so would bring you riches and happiness beyond measure?

Positive goals and grand visions are compelling: you looking fit and gorgeous in a red dress or a sharp suit, you running a marathon, you glowing with health from the inside out. "Eating more beans" is a less compelling vision. Remember that a goal you can picture is worth 1,000 words, so now collect pictures that inspire you to move toward your goal and stick them into a book or put them on a pin board (real or virtual). Collect beautiful images of healthy food, peaceful scenes, or calm and mindful activities, and make it as real as possible for you. Go and hang out in the gym, create an altar or creative table in your house for what you want; get organized by following the steps that we suggest a bit later on in this chapter, such as clearing out junk and filling your cupboards with beautiful containers for healthy food. **Create space for it and it will come.**

Write down your three most important goals now. Pick one and make a big vibrant image of the end result you want. When you have achieved that goal, what will you see, hear, and feel? Make a mind-movie of yourself reaching your goal. **See yourself as the star of that movie.** Make your movie wild, wonderful, fun, crazy, limitless. Imagine everything you want to happen coming true, everyone standing up and cheering you on everywhere you go. Is that really any less plausible than the negative things you worry might happen?

The difference between a dream and a goal is an action plan

Taking Action

The difference between a dream and a goal is an action plan. If you plan to take action, however small, toward your goal on a daily basis, you will get where you want to be in no time at all. You may not be able to climb Everest today, but you can buy yourself the boots. Planning to do something, then actually doing it, lets your unconscious mind know that you mean business, and once it understands that, it will marshal your resources to help you. Buy a beautiful journal and write your goals in it as this will make your aims more concrete.

CONTRACT

I (insert your name)...
commit to taking the following actions to accomplish my goals:

I will...

I will...

I will...

Sign and date:..

FOOD FOR THOUGHT

Once you have noted your goals in a compelling form in your journal, decide on some actions you could take now. Make a "to-do" list that will show commitment to the end result you want. This might be something as simple as reading an article, making a phone call, setting the table. A great thing to do would be to tell a friend or colleague about your goal or create a way to track it. This puts positive pressure on you to stick to your plan and make it happen.

If the thought of writing a to-do list produces less than ecstatic feelings in you, make it fun. Brighten your list (and your day) by interspersing it with some "to-dos" that raise your spirits.

Today's to-do list:

Organize and de-junk my kitchen cupboards

Give myself a healthy treat

Sing

Laugh out loud every hour

Stop and compliment myself on what a great job I'm doing

Daydream about something wonderful happening

Make sure you tick them all off.

What Gets Measured Gets Done

Use the journal you bought for yourself, or go out and buy one if you haven't done so already, and **begin tracking your food intake** and thought-observations daily. The idea is that this journal will accompany you throughout the process, so do spend time choosing one that you will love to carry around with you. You may have heard the phrase **"what gets measured gets done,"** and this sums up beautifully why we encourage you to use a journal daily as part of your journey into mindful eating. The simple act of tracking your own progress has a huge part to play in how successful you will be when it comes to changing your eating habits. Writing in a journal keeps you sharply focused on your actions; it is difficult to mindlessly ignore the fact that you are eating fast food on the run when you know you will later have to write this down.

From a practical point of view, your journal is a space for you to **note down everything that you eat** and drink each day. Write down where and how you eat and drink, for example, did you eat quickly at your desk or in a relaxed way at a table? In addition, use this space to note down your observations about food, to check in on how you are feeling. Jot down ideas that may arise and thoughts that come up as you work through the simple "food for thought" exercises.

Keeping a journal allows you to focus sharply on your actions and plays a huge part in helping you to change your eating habits.

Get Organized

People who successfully maintain healthy eating habits are typically very **organized about food**, and this, like any other habit, is one **you can learn**. We like to think that these practical "getting organized" steps are rather like laying the table before a meal, or preparing a vegetable bed before you plant the seedlings. When you take steps to become more organized about food, you are laying the perfect foundations for success.

Spring-clean your space—it's essential that your cooking and dining areas are lovely spaces to in which to spend time. You don't need to invest in a brand new kitchen or re-decorate, you simply need to **re-organize your space to make it more inviting**. **Clear out your kitchen cabinets**, clean out your refrigerator, and throw out any pots and pans, cups, and plates you no longer want to use, along with anything you no longer wish to eat. You are making space for new foods and your new approach to cooking and eating. Open the windows and let in some fresh air, clean out a vase, add some fresh water and fresh flowers, light a scented candle, choose your favourite tablecloth, and finally set out the placemats.

Organize your kitchen cabinets, refrigerator, and freezer—once you've had a chance to sort through what you do and do not want to keep and finished your spring clean, it's time to **invest in some new containers** so you can store, organize, and label dry food items such as cereals, nuts, seeds, pulses, lentils, rice, oatmeal, grains, herbs, and spices. There are many storage companies/kitchen supply stores who do a great range of differently sized, stackable products, so it's well worth a shopping trip or online search to get you started. **Make sure your cabinets, refrigerator, and freezer are clean and organized** so that everything is easy to find, labeled, and easily accessible. Make it your own with customized labels and an injection of your personality.

Organize pots and pans—check that you have a good range of different sized pots, casserole dishes, a skillet, wok, roasting pan, and baking trays.

Stock up on portable and freezable storage containers—most superstores now do a good range of portable containers that you can use to carry lunch and snacks. Glass containers are better for your health, but plastic ones are often more practical; **choose whichever best suits your lifestyle**. Stock up on freezable containers in different sizes, too, so you can easily freeze portions of soups, casseroles, and sauces.

Portable water bottle—it's so much easier to get into the habit of drinking more water if you have it with you all the time. Invest in a good-quality portable water bottle and take it with you everywhere.

Food flask—a food flask is invaluable for taking soups, one pot meals, or hot beany dips to work or out and about with you. You will find food flasks widely available in a variety of sizes online.

Buy yourself a gorgeous lunch bag—you'll feel much more like organizing your lunch in advance if you have a beautiful lunch bag to fill, so go on, have a look at what's out there and treat yourself to something you'll love.

Have a "time" audit—being organized and eating mindfully takes time. We can't add extra hours to each day so it's important to be clear now, at the outset, where this time will come from (rather than just crossing your fingers and hoping for the best).

Have a look at your typical weekly schedule—identify some activities that no longer fit with your goals and plan, instead, to allocate this time to nurturing your new mindful habits. Plan your time for shopping, preparing, and cooking food, and eating your meals. You may only be able to re-allocate a little time to begin with, but don't be disheartened, this is perfectly normal. We encourage you to audit your time regularly throughout this process.

Find a mindful buddy or set up a group—something magical happens when two or more people come together to support each other. You may want to enjoy this journey on your own, or you may decide that you'll work best as part of a team, with a buddy, or even perhaps a bigger group. Decide what will work best for you and take action now to make it happen.

Some mindful thoughts to contemplate

Your mind and body are inextricably linked. Working with the two simultaneously brings the best results.

Your body is paying attention to everything you say, so your inner monologue about what's possible and right for you will make the difference between living mindfully and mindlessly.

You have a conscious and an unconscious mind and they work best as a team.

The time you invest in building a great relationship with your inner wisdom (your unconscious mind) will reap great rewards.

You are in charge of making the changes you want to make and you can draw on a tremendous storehouse of unconscious resources to get there.

You always have the choice to change.

Failure, judgment, and deprivation mindsets lead to more of the same.

Talk to yourself like you would talk to your best friend (some people talk to themselves in a way they would never speak to anyone else). Be kind to yourself and you will notice more things that are good about you.

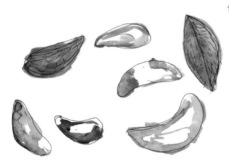

CHORIZO, CHICKPEAS, LENTILS, AND GREENS

This is a great recipe to start with if you're not used to cooking with beans and lentils. It is so tasty that it immediately dispels any myths about lentils being bland and boring. This deliciously hearty soup is a meal in itself and makes a perfect lunch or midweek supper. Recipe courtesy of Riverford Organic (www.riverford.co.uk.)

3½oz/100g puy lentils

2 tbsp oil

3oz/75g cooking chorizo, chopped (leave this out for a vegetarian alternative)

1 onion, peeled and chopped

2 cloves garlic, peeled and crushed, or finely chopped

2 tsp ground cumin

2 tsp ground cilantro/coriander

⅓ tsp ground cinnamon

¼–½ tsp dried chili flakes

4 fresh tomatoes, chopped, or use ½ can tomatoes

14oz/400g can chickpeas, rinsed and drained

5 cups/1.2 liters chicken or vegetable stock

½ head of chard, leaves shredded, stalks finely chopped

Salt and pepper

Juice of ½ lemon

Serves 4

Put the lentils in a large saucepan, add water to cover, bring to boil and simmer for 20 minutes or until tender. Drain. Heat the oil, then fry the chorizo (if using), onion, and garlic. Add spices and chili and fry for a couple more minutes. Add the tomatoes, chickpeas, chard, and stock. Bring to a boil, then simmer for 15 minutes. Add the lentils back to the pan and continue to simmer for a couple of minutes until they are warmed through. Season with salt and pepper. Add lemon juice to taste.

Future Self Meditation

Focus your attention on one of your goals. Ask yourself how real it is for you on a scale from 1–10.

Sit down somewhere quiet and begin to bring your attention to the now by focusing on your breathing. Use the time it takes to settle and become relaxed, then connect to a source of light which can be whatever color you wish. Imagine that it radiates into you and through you, getting stronger with every breath, until it gradually begins to extend beyond you to all the people and places around you, with every breath expanding more, to the stars and beyond. Imagine that with your newfound light you can illuminate everything around you and connect to anywhere you want to go—to the stars, to the past, and even to your future. Look at your future—see where it stretches out in front of you. Imagine you are easily and effortlessly able to find the place in the future where you will have achieved your goals, and where you are experiencing the wonderful feelings that result from your accomplishments. See your future self, glowing with the bright light of success, sparkling and glittering and basking in it. Notice what you are doing, what you are saying to yourself, you could even be aware of the soundtrack of success playing in the background. Notice once again how you are connected to everything around you and that when you succeed, the impact spreads out like the ripples in a pond to benefit your whole future, the futures of all those around you, and of generations to come. See the way it will be of great benefit to the whole of the planet and beyond. Ask your future self what it took to get to this place of success and integrate the knowledge you need to take those steps. Now, when you're ready, step into the future you and experience all those great feelings and that knowledge from the inside in the now. You can stay there for as long as it takes to begin fully absorbing those thoughts and feelings into your awareness so that you can bring them back to the present, fully motivated to take the first step. Take time to learn and experience whatever you need to move towards your future as you enjoy breathing those feelings into your body. Step out of the future you and know that your self has something to give you to remind you of this experience. Take this gift from the future you, noticing what kind of object or shape it is—what color and form it takes—see the gift infused with the energy of your goal. Put it somewhere safe so that you can access this resource any time you want in the future.

Then, on a breath that feels right, get ready to connect to your light again and gradually bring yourself back to this time, this location, and to your breathing in the time it takes to integrate your new feelings and knowledge into the you of here and now. Come back to now, aware of the present, and ready to start on your path to the future.

Now you're back, take a few breaths, stretch and plant your feet firmly back on the ground. When you're fully back, rate your feelings about achieving your goal on a scale of 1–10 again. Let your gift from the future guide you towards the right actions to achieve your goals from today.

Chapter 4

Changing Your Habits

The Glade

A troupe of pixies lived in a wooded glade very close to a well-traveled path. Pixies are so small and fast that you usually can't see them, even if you are looking for them. This made life easy for the mischievous pixies, who enjoyed playing tricks on the local people. They particularly liked to set gossamer tripwires and dug holes so that the locals would stumble and fall.

A woman named Lizzie was one such local. She walked her dog past the pixies every day and always fell victim to their pranks. Her faithful dog could sense that the pixies were nearby and he tried to call her attention to their traps, but she paid no heed.

One day Lizzie tripped over a gossamer thread, fell, and hit her head on a tree trunk. When she woke up, she realized that a group of pixies were staring at her with great interest. She quickly stood up and told herself that she must be mistaken. But, deep down, she knew that the pixies were real.

Over the course of the next week, Lizzie covered her eyes as she walked through the glade, or she simply didn't go out at all. Then she had a life-changing thought: she could not avoid the pixies, but if she allowed herself to see them, she could avoid their traps.

During her next walk, she paid attention to her surroundings. She saw the pixies and was able to stay one step ahead of their pranks. She also noticed that her dog would warn her in advance if there were pixies nearby.

Soon she took different routes and found creative paths around the pixies. Within weeks she learned to laugh at their antics and although they still occasionally caught her out, she was usually able to remain mindful and do things differently.

Become a Mindful Detective

"The definition of insanity is doing the same thing over and over again and expecting different results."

Albert Einstein

We are all creatures of habit, and habits are powerful things. We want you to **become a mindful detective** about your current eating habits. If you start to be really curious about your habitual food-related patterns, you become aware enough to choose whether to keep or change them. Nothing can change without awareness, and once **you are mindful of what you're doing** you will never do it in quite the same way as before. Try eating some cookies or other junk food while staring at yourself in the mirror. Not quite as much fun is it? What would happen if you did this every day?

We want you to think about all of your current habits. All of these habits—even the bad ones — prove that **you can learn** something and replicate it perfectly without ever getting it wrong. If you can do that, you can put your mind to learning all kinds of other useful skills. Stop judging yourself for your habits and choose curiosity about them instead. Judgment closes you down and locks you into position; it is the enemy of change. When you judge or criticize yourself you're unlikely to **be in a resourceful place**, and therefore unlikely to **be open to creative solutions**. Change requires you to **feel positive, open, and creative**. Make friends with curiosity because it creates those states.

FOOD FOR THOUGHT

Rediscover your curiosity

Close your eyes for a moment and remember a time when you were really curious. Perhaps this is when you were a child on Christmas morning. What do you remember? How did it feel to open the door and see the beautiful gifts under the tree? Did you imagine all of the wonderful things that might be inside? Or maybe it's how you feel when you just can't put down a book because you are so desperate to know how it ends. Think about these feelings of curiosity. Note down in your journal times in your life when you have felt truly curious about something. Hold on to a feeling of curiosity as you explore your habits in this chapter.

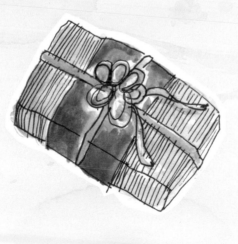

Changing habits

Once a behavior is learned and repeated several times, **your unconscious mind does it for you. It's virtually effortless.** This goes for good habits (brushing your teeth, going to the gym, meditating, preparing healthy food) as well as unwanted ones (snacking on chips and cookies, eating take-out).

You don't usually **think about your habits** because they are the norm for you. If you were to observe someone else (perhaps a roommate or family member) you would **become aware that what you do is one option among many.** The food habits that you engage in on a daily basis will be largely automatic, usually learned in childhood, and repeated until they became the norm.

When we practice habitual behaviors we operate in a kind of trance. Just look around a coffee shop sometime and you'll notice many people in "eating trances." They may be mindlessly shoveling food into their mouths with glazed eyes while talking, watching television, playing on their phones, or reading a paper, completely unconscious of what they are eating.

It's important to know that there are useful habits as well as negative ones. It's helpful to be able to do many everyday activities automatically. Habits become problematic when they cause harmful mindless behavior.

You may see the need to clear out your cabinets and revamp your wardrobe but do you ever **take the time to de-clutter your mind of habits that no longer serve you?**

Once a pattern is automated it often continues unless something drastic happens to make you reconsider. This could be an ultimatum from the doctor or your weight creeping up on the scales. Why not stop and think now without a crisis? You could choose to put yourself in the driver's seat right now and let go of your unwanted habits.

FOOD FOR THOUGHT

What are your eating habits?

Use your journal to make a note of them.

Some common daily eating habits that we often hear about are:

Being an auto-condimentalist—this sounds grand but simply means you add salt and pepper to your food without tasting it first.

Eating the same thing every day for breakfast—e.g. toast.

Having a cookie with a cup of coffee.

Eating bread with a meal.

Having sugar in your tea.

Skipping breakfast.

Finishing a meal with something sweet.

Eating snacks while watching television.

Having a glass of wine with pasta.

Now think about where these habits came from. What eating habits and rules did you learn from your family? Did you pick up any food habits at school? Did you learn to eat quickly or slowly? What kind of food did you see as a treat/as a punishment or a chore? What foods were appropriate to have for breakfast? Did you learn to finish eating when you were full or when your plate was clean? When were your mealtimes? Were you taught that every meal ends with a dessert?

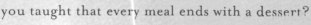

Which habits would you like to let go of now?

Changing habits can feel less than comfortable because you've practiced them for so long, but what you have learned can be unlearned and replaced with something more positive. Habits may feel like they are hard-wired, but just remember that you had to **practice them to learn** them in the first place. When you were born, you didn't just get up and walk; you learned to walk step by step. You mastered holding yourself upright, then you discovered how to move and crawl, you pulled yourself up on the furniture, and finally took your first tentative steps. Now you don't have to think about how to stand up—you **just decide to and it happens.**

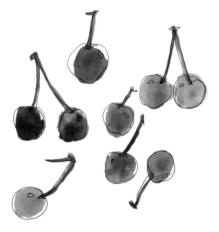

Although habits can feel like they are single units of behavior, in fact they are complex sequences of actions with beginnings, middles, and endings. Take "eating a morning snack" as an example. It is triggered by something that could be external (looking at a clock) or internal (a thought or feeling). You then go through the middle process of choosing and eating your snack and the end comes when something lets you know **it's time to stop eating.** During all these stages you may be mindfully aware or in a mindless trance. The first step to changing a habit is to **slow down and become mindful of it. When you know the habits that you want to change,** you can use the following strategies to let go and replace them with positive new ones.

Know Your Triggers

How do you know when to start eating? Triggers for eating can be external, internal, or a combination of both. People often tell us they start eating because of an external trigger:

* The clock strikes twelve or someone suggests it's time to eat.

* Someone offers me some food or puts it in front of me.

* I see something delicious at the store.

* I see an advertisement on television.

* I smell a tempting aroma from a shop.

We are also bombarded by external food cues in our environment. You only need to walk through the nearest shopping precinct to see countless signs advertising food in all forms. Everything we see and hear has an impact on our unconscious mind at some level. We respond particularly well to pictures and the food industry knows this only too well. Superstores bombard all our senses with tempting aromas and mouth-watering pictures as soon as we walk in the door. They put the "impulse buys" at eye level and create colorful displays. Before you know it, you start to feel hungry.

There are also numerous internal triggers. Thoughts about food often trigger eating. If you start to think about your favorite dessert in glorious Technicolor and begin to imagine the way it smells and tastes, you will be running to the refrigerator in no time.

When **you are on the lookout for your triggers you can begin to change them significantly.** Once you recognize a trigger, **you have a moment of choice.** It is up to you to seize that moment to make a new decision.

Knowing the way your mind works can help you to **make it work for you.** It is widely accepted that people eat a lot more when food is visible. The harder food is to obtain, even if the extra effort involves just removing a lid or walking to the cabinet, the less likely you are to eat it. To **avoid snacking on the foods you'd rather not eat regularly, keep them out of sight**, or better yet, out of the house.

Create a positive trigger by keeping healthy foods prominently displayed and easy to reach. Make sure you have plenty of healthy snacks including fresh fruit and vegetables in the kitchen. Make this delicious, healthy food visually appealing by leaving mouth-watering pictures of tasty, nutrient-packed meals around the house.

Keep healthy foods prominently displayed and easy to reach.

Make Every Meal Special

Meals can be spread over many courses and many hours. In our "lunch is for wimps" culture we can often make a virtue out of devouring food as quickly as possible, eating at our desk, or grabbing a snack and getting back to work. As far as we are concerned, however, **anything worth eating is worth making a meal over.** Even the simplest dinner should be a cornucopia of different tastes and textures. You have five different senses for a reason: aim for each meal to satisfy as many of them as possible and you will feel truly sated. **You can make every meal a special occasion even if you are short on time.** Lay the table, even if you're on your own, and celebrate the lovely, healthy food to which you are treating your body. **Present the food beautifully and enjoy every mouthful.**

FOOD FOR THOUGHT

Before you begin eating, sit and appreciate the food with your eyes. Look at the variety of colors, see the different shapes and textures. Inhale the aromas of the food as you begin to take some deep breaths into your belly, relaxing into a calm state that is perfect for digesting your food. Close your eyes as you start to imagine how the food will taste when you eat it. Imagine experiencing each flavor exploding in your mouth as it hits the different taste buds. Eat a forkful of food and then put down your silverware. Close your eyes and totally focus on the flavors. Chew thoroughly, imagining how this wonderful food is nourishing your body and mind, and feeling it benefiting all of your systems. Listen to your body and stop eating when you begin to feel pleasantly full. Research shows that people who are blindfolded eat much less than people who can see their food, because they are able to truly focus on their body's signals.

Know When to Stop Eating

It seems simple that you should stop when you've had enough, but often people have grown up with the "clean plate club" mentality; if there's anything left there's still work to do. Most young children won't overeat naturally, but instincts can be overridden. Prizes for clean plates are still given at some schools and if this happened to you it may have taken you out of sync with the innate wisdom of your body, which will naturally tell you when to stop.

Our society also tends to see over-feeding people as a way to nurture them. It is a form of pressure, which is seen as socially acceptable.

Are there times you feel pressured to eat even when you're full? Most of us have automatically eaten the children's leftover chicken nuggets simply because we don't want to waste them. An interesting experiment found that people offered buckets of popcorn in a cinema mindlessly ate through them no matter what size they were given and continued to eat even when the popcorn was stale—simply because it was there. The message in this is that we need to **be mindful and take back control** of our eating. We want you to **eat exactly what you want, when you want it.** There is no forbidden food or self-denial, but we want you to **be in charge of what you eat** and when, so that you can make the best choices for yourself.

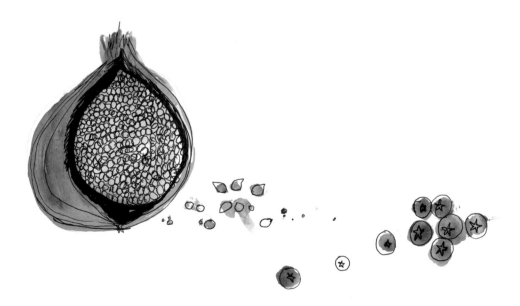

Pay Attention to Your Hunger Signals

"There is more wisdom in your body than in your deepest philosophies."

Friedrich Nietzsche

It's important to learn to read and **trust your body's signals.** Just as babies have different cries for being hungry, wet, or calling for attention, we have different bodily signals that could all be read as hunger. Begin to **listen to your different cries** and find out what you are really hungry for.

Next time you want to eat, pause, breathe deeply, and begin to focus on your belly. Ask yourself how hungry you are on a scale of one to ten. If you're at a one, two, or three it's likely you are just eating out of habit. Think of something else you could do and do it right now (perhaps have a glass of water). Keep checking in with yourself and eat when you really do feel hungry (five, six, or seven). Avoid getting up to an eight, nine, or ten. We want you to begin to understand what "hungry" actually feels like (though not so hungry that you will eat anything!).

Be in charge of what you eat and when, so that you can make the best choices for yourself.

Interrupt Your Habits

Another great way to **loosen the grip of a habit** is to **interrupt it as soon as you become aware of it.** When a pattern is altered it starts to fall apart. You would **come out of a mindless eating trance** naturally if you noticed something unexpected on your plate, but you can also break the trance deliberately. You have changed many habits in the past both consciously and unconsciously. Once a habit is interrupted, it begins to fall away.

There are many ways to **deliberately interrupt an unwanted pattern**, but our favorite one is laughter. One of our course participants had a mindless post-lunch chocolate-cookie habit at work. We encouraged her to stand up and announce to the whole office, "I am now about to eat another chocolate cookie." It made her laugh every time she thought about it and she never even got close to making the announcement—the habit soon changed. Some people have put signs on the refrigerator saying, "I have a choice," others like to visualize a stop sign or shout, "Do I want this?" at the critical moment. You can **make a habit of breaking habits.**

Dare To Do Something Different

Personally, we like to **change at least one habit every month.** This is because **all change is generative.** Every time you **change something in your life,** however small, you are giving yourself the empowering message that **you can change. Change generates more change.** So **start small and you will find that it can lead to some astonishing new possibilities** for you. We have been amazed at just how many major life changes people have made once they start to take steps to change their eating habits. Once you realize you can do it, the sky really is the limit. Let's start to consciously tell your brain that change is possible. Set yourself a challenge to do something outside your comfort zone. Do something totally different with food this week. For example:

- Try a new food or food combination

- Break a food taboo: have some chocolate-covered vegetables or shrimp!

- Eat with your fingers or use chopsticks.

FOOD FOR THOUGHT

Soup and ?

For most people, soup is served with bread or crackers. This is one habit that we like to challenge simply because people often find it easy to eat too much bread. Soup is a fabulous way to consume a wide variety of different vegetables. It's easy (you can cook it in big batches in advance and freeze it in individual portions), it's portable (get yourself a food flask and you can take it to work with you), and you can make it complex by adding meat, poultry, fish, beans, lentils, garbanzo beans, and a huge range of other tasty ingredients. We love soup. However, we encourage you to start challenging the habit of having bread or crackers with your soup, instead, have an accompanying salad, or even just the soup on its own.

Do Breakfast Differently

Ask yourself now: what would be the easiest thing you could do differently that would make the most impact on your life if you were to do it consistently? Breakfast is a great place to start.

For many people, breakfast is a habitual cup of coffee, sometimes accompanied by a slice of toast or a bowl of sugary breakfast cereal. People tend to have a fixed idea of what foods are permitted at breakfast time and will often have the same thing every day. While we're not suggesting that you have to start each day with a hot and spicy curry or a colorful salad, when you try out some unusual breakfasts, you will **send your brain the message that you can do things differently**, propelling forward the process of change.

Starting tomorrow, challenge yourself to make time for a relaxed breakfast every day for a week. Why not up the stakes and have a different breakfast each day, including at least three unusual breakfasts? (Hint: planning ahead and getting organized is key to your success in this challenge, so make your weekly breakfast plan now.)

Some ideas for a mindful breakfast with a difference:

* **Breakfast mish-mash hash—gently fry some finely chopped red onion and garlic; add a handful of chopped mushrooms and cherry tomatoes, a couple of handfuls of spinach, and half a can of garbanzo beans; heat through and serve, topped with plenty of freshly ground black pepper, a light sprinkle of parmesan, and sunflower seeds.**

* **Melon with serrano ham and sliced mozzarella.**

* **Grilled mackerel, sliced beefsteak tomato, and steamed tenderstem broccoli.**

It takes about a month to **create a new habit**, but **once you've created it, you can let it run.** Repetition is the key. One of our course participants took this a little to the extreme. He hated olives but wanted to like them. He made himself eat 100 of them over a month on the grounds that if you eat anything often enough, your tastebuds will become accustomed to it. Hey presto, he now likes olives.

Get Creative with Salads

Many people tell us they "don't like salad." However, we usually discover that it's the bit of limp lettuce, cucumber, and sliced tomato on the side of a plate that they struggle to get excited about. Boring, tasteless salads often referred to as "rabbit food" or "diet food" are more commonly seen than exciting, delicious ones. Salads have become synonymous with dieting and deprivation, so many people rebel against this by making a habit of avoiding them.

We would like you to challenge your own habits when it comes to eating salads. Ask yourself what ingredients you can put into a salad and note down your typical list. Ask yourself: When is it okay to eat a salad? Can you eat salad in the winter? Can you mix hot and cold foods in a salad? Can you add fruit to a salad? Do you enjoy eating salad?

The next step is to start a new habit of making salads, which will have your friends and colleagues green with envy. We want you to enter the delicious world of super salads.

Start thinking differently about salads. Discover the delicious world of super salads.

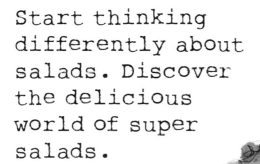

THE SUPER SALAD

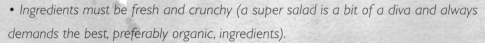

- *Ingredients must be fresh and crunchy (a super salad is a bit of a diva and always demands the best, preferably organic, ingredients).*
- *A plate of lettuce does not constitute a salad, but a salad may contain some lettuce (use rocket instead of iceberg lettuce, and lollo rosso in place of flat lettuce to make things even more interesting).*
- *Super salads contain a brightly colored mix of fruit and vegetables, some high-quality protein such as lean red meat, chicken, tofu, fish, beans, or pulses, and some beneficial fat in the form of nuts, seeds and their oils, oily fish, home-made salad dressing, avocado, or olives. The super salad is a complex creature.*
- *You can put anything into a super salad; never underestimate just how much difference a handful of pomegranate seeds, some grated fennel, fresh herbs, ripe peach slices, or a few anchovies can make to the taste of your salad. Think outside the (Tupperware) box for best results.*
- *A super salad takes a while to eat. You can't eat a super salad on the go; you have to make some time to sit and mindfully enjoy this attention-craving creation.*
- *A super salad can be eaten in the spring, summer, fall, and winter; it isn't a hedgehog and doesn't hibernate.*
- *No two super salads are ever the same; yours will be filled with your personality. Make your plate your own.*
- *Others will be envious of your super salad and this will confuse them, as they have never before desired a salad so much. Never leave it unattended or you may find it mysteriously vanishes.*

Now it's time to get creative and make your own super salad.

SLOW-COOKED LAMB SALAD WITH BEANS, POMEGRANATE, AND FRESH MINT

Let all of your senses feast on the preparation and enjoyment of this delicious super salad.
Do something different and try it as a lovely alternative to a traditional Sunday roast.

2 tbsp light olive oil

1 tbsp sea salt

1 tbsp ground cumin

4 lbs/2 kg bone-in lamb shoulder

1 lb/500g fresh young fava/broad beans

Leaves from a bunch of fresh mint

Seeds from 1 pomegranate

2 tbsp extra-virgin olive oil

2 tbsp freshly squeezed lemon juice

Sea salt and freshly ground black pepper

Serves 6

Preheat the oven to 325°F (160°C)/Gas 3. Rub the extra-virgin olive oil and the salt and cumin all over the lamb. Sit the lamb on a rack placed over a large baking sheet. Cook in the preheated oven for 6 hours. Remove, lightly cover with foil, and let rest for up to 3 hours. Cook the fava/broad beans in a large saucepan of boiling water for 10 minutes, until just tender. Drain well. Use a fork or your fingers to shred the lamb off the bone. Transfer to a bowl and add the fava/broad beans, mint leaves, pomegranate seeds, extra-virgin olive oil, and lemon juice. Toss to combine, and season to taste with salt and pepper.

SPICED PUMPKIN, SPELT, AND GOAT CHEESE SALAD

This recipe is a lovely reminder of lazy days spent lingering over wonderfully nutritious and delicious salads in sunny Sydney. Why not make a lantern and bake the pumpkin seeds too?

⅓ cup/50g whole spelt

14oz/400g peeled and deseeded pumpkin

¼ cup/65ml olive oil

½ teaspoon sea salt

½ tsp Spanish smoked sweet paprika
(pimentón dulce)

¼ tsp dried chili/hot pepper flakes

¼ tsp ground allspice

⅓ cup/50g unsalted cashew nuts

1 tbsp white wine vinegar

4oz/100g soft goat cheese

4 handfuls of wild arugula/rocket

Freshly ground black pepper

Serves 4

Put the spelt in a large saucepan with plenty of boiling water. Set over high heat, bring back to the boil, Cook for about 30 minutes, until just tender. Drain well and set aside. Preheat the oven to 350°F (180°C)/Gas 4. Cut the pumpkin flesh into large chunks and put in a bowl with the oil, salt, paprika, chili/hot pepper flakes, and allspice. Toss to coat the pumpkin in the spiced oil. Tumble the pumpkin onto the prepared baking sheet and pour over any spiced oil from the bowl. Cook in the preheated oven for 20 minutes. Remove from the over, scatter over the cashews, and return to the oven for a further 8–10 minutes, until the cashews are golden. Remove from the oven and set aside. Combine the remaining oil and vinegar in a small bowl. Put the spelt, spiced pumpkin, cashews, goat cheese, and arugula/rocket in a large bowl and gently toss to combine, being careful not to break up the cheese or pumpkin too much. Pour over the dressing and season with black pepper. Serve immediately.

Mindfully Take Control

Start with the end in mind. What habits would you like to let go of or acquire? What would you like to experience more of in your life—health, happiness, mindfulness? Pay attention to your breathing and **still your mind.** We are going on a journey of inner discovery to visit the place in your brain that is the control center for all your thoughts and feelings. Find yourself at this center, look around, and explore it. This is the place where you can **take charge of your inner states, your thoughts, your feelings, your health, your sensations, and your habits.** Put yourself in the driver's seat and prepare to switch to manual. Have a good look at the dashboard in front of you—there may be lights, gauges, buttons, switches, dials, and levers, all with various functions. One might be health, another happiness, confidence, self-control, relaxation, or whatever it is you want more of in your life. **Begin to adjust the settings.** You might see numbers change as you do this. You may find a manual nearby to help you find the correct settings for perfect health and happiness. Perhaps you even have some technical assistance at hand to guide you through what you need to do. Anything that helps you will be right there when you need it; just help yourself. Each time you adjust a setting on the dashboard fully experience the change in your body— experience that boost in confidence or that glow of health, and fully immerse yourself in those sensations. **Breathe in the good feelings** and enjoy the amplification of all that is right within you. Before you leave your control center, **reflect on the day ahead**, and imagine yourself moving through your day more positively now that you've made these changes

Chapter 5

The Principles of Mindful Eating

The Rainbow

Once upon a time, all the colors in the world started to vie for superiority. They argued all day long, each one claiming that it was the most important. Green said, "I am clearly the best color in the world. I am the primary color in nature; I paint the meadows, the leaves, and the vegetation." Blue interrupted, "I am the sea and the sky, the calm peaceful backdrop to all that is." Red exploded at that, "I am fire and passion. Without me there would be no contrast." "Oh please," interrupted Orange, "I bring the warmth of hearth and home without the need for temper." "Get over yourselves," laughed Yellow, "I bring the rays of the sun and put a smile on everyone's face with my warmth and light." Indigo refused to shout with the others to make herself heard and, with quiet composure, she stated her case, "My deep waters and dark nights bring silence and deep truth to the world." Purple pulled himself to his full height and took center stage, "I am the color of kings and ceremony; the highest and most spiritual of all colors."

Suddenly, there was a clap of thunder and a bolt of lightning, and rain began to pour down in torrents on the colors, drowning out all the squabbling. The colors came closer together for protection, forming a band that spread out across the sky. Rain began to speak, "Why are you fighting with one another? Look how amazing it is when you all come together, each in your place, each with a different purpose, blending your unique qualities into a rainbow of hope."

The colors listened to Rain and realized that he was right. They remembered his wisdom and shone that little bit brighter from then on.

What is a Healthy Diet?

With so many different versions of a "healthy diet" out there, you would be forgiven for wondering how best to nourish your body. We offer a down-to-earth version of what constitutes a healthy, balanced diet—a simple set of nutrition principles, with no gimmicks and no fads.

Michael Pollan perfectly summarizes a healthy diet in just seven words. In his eater's manifesto—*In Defence of Food*—he says: **"Eat food. Not too much. Mostly plants."** Make a note of this and stick it on your refrigerator.

Many people are overfed and undernourished. Paradoxical and even absurd as this may sound, this is what the "Western diet" typically delivers. Our nutrition principles encourage you to **choose food mindfully that will leave you well fed and optimally nourished.** Real food has so much to offer to your health and well-being, and we want to help you **channel all of this goodness into the best version of you.** You've set your compelling goals and imagined what they look like, you've become more organized and made space for all these fabulous new foods. You've chosen to **make you your number one priority** and have started the process of changing negative habits. Now it's time to learn the principles of mindful eating.

These principles **work best when you take the time to think about** and really understand them, not just superficially, but at a deeper level too.

Underpinning each principle is a strong support system, just like a plant's network of roots. We encourage you to take your time to engage with each principle as you will then have something long-lasting that will grow and flourish for many years to come.

Take your time to **savor each principle individually before moving on to the next one**, just as you would with the courses of a delicious meal. Know that real, sustainable change takes time. There is no rush.

Mindfully choose food that will leave you well fed and optimally nourished.

ASPARAGUS, CHIVE,
AND PEA SHOOT OMELET

*One of the joys of keeping hens is the daily hunt for their nutritious gifts. Eggs are
a wonderful, complete food and an easy, fairly inexpensive way to add some high-quality
protein to your diet. Choose organic and free-range eggs for the best results. Used as
a breakfast recipe, this delicious omelet will be a great start to your day.*

14oz/400g fava/broad beans

9oz/250g asparagus, trimmed

4 tsp olive oil

8 eggs

1 generous cup/125g crumbled soft goat cheese

3½oz/100g pea shoots

4 tbsp chopped fresh chives

Sea salt and ground black pepper

Serves 4

Steam the fava beans and asparagus for 4 minutes or until the
vegetables are tender. Set the asparagus aside. Gently squeeze the
beans out of their gray outer shell. Set aside with the asparagus.
Heat the oil in a nonstick frying pan. Lightly beat 2 of the eggs,
season with salt and pepper, and pour them into the pan. Tip the
pan until the egg mixture coats the base. Cook for 2–3 minutes
then slip the flat omelet onto a serving plate.
Put a quarter of the goat cheese in the center of the omelet. Top with
a quarter of the fava beans, asparagus, and pea shoots. Sprinkle with
some chives before serving. Repeat to make three more omelets.

HERRING WITH BEETS ON SOURDOUGH RYE

Packed full of beneficial fats, bright color, and variety, this simple recipe ticks all the nutrition boxes and looks and tastes divine.

8 herring fillets

Extra-virgin olive oil, for brushing and drizzling

Juice of 1 lemon

8 slices sourdough rye bread

8 soft lettuce leaves

2in/5cm piece cucumber, thinly sliced into rounds

3 cooked beets/beetroot in natural juice, diced

½ small red onion, diced

Sea salt and ground black pepper

Small sprigs of fresh dill to garnish

Serves 4

Preheat the broiler (grill) to high and line the broiler pan with foil. Lightly brush the foil with oil. Arrange the herring fillets skin-side up in the pan and squeeze over half the lemon juice. Season, then broil (grill) the fish for 3–4 minutes until cooked through.

Meanwhile, put 2 slices of bread on each serving plate and top with a lettuce leaf and a few slices of cucumber. Mix together the beets and red onion. Put a herring fillet on each slice of bread. Top with the beets and onion, squeeze over the remaining lemon juice and add a drizzle of olive oil. Serve topped with a few sprigs of dill.

The Mindful Eating Principles

1 Eat three smaller meals and three snacks daily. Avoid becoming ravenously hungry. Aim to eat every 2–3 hours.

Many people are engaged in a constant battle to eat less food, less often. Yet just like a car, your body needs regular pit stops to refuel and keep it running efficiently. For your body, that fuel is food and water. From food, **your amazing body produces energy** and extracts essential nutrients. You will get a better performance out of a car by using high-quality fuel; similarly, **your body will reward regular meals and snacks and high-quality nutrition** with vibrant health and well-being. Aim to eat every 2–3 hours and avoid becoming ravenously hungry.

2 Choose whole, unprocessed foods, which are as close to their natural state as possible.

When you choose to follow these principles, you will experience natural blood-sugar balance as a result. "Blood sugar" literally refers to sugar in your blood and this is what your body uses to make energy throughout the day. Your blood-sugar level is determined by everything that you eat and drink, and lifestyle factors such as activity level, sleep quality, and stress. It can be harmful to your health if your blood-sugar levels rise too high or dip too low and your body has a set of internal mechanisms to keep the levels within a safe range.

✳ If blood sugar is too high, your body sends out a hormone called insulin to bring it back down.

✳ If blood sugar is too low, your body will initiate cravings for sugary foods or drinks to help bring levels back up.

A typical Western diet high in refined processed meals, sugary drinks and snacks, stimulants, alcohol, and stress plays havoc with blood-sugar levels. This means that your body must constantly intervene to balance them. This daily blood-sugar rollercoaster is associated with symptoms such as low

energy, mood swings, irritability, low concentration, poor sleep, and cravings for caffeine, alcohol, and sugar. Do any of these symptoms sound familiar? You can mindfully choose to eat and live in a way that naturally supports blood sugar balance and by doing so, you will soon feel positive effects on your health. Use whole, unprocessed foods and cook from scratch as often as possible. Choose to eat organic, free-range, and seasonally as much as you can. Keeping your blood-sugar levels balanced will lead to high energy, reduced cravings, great sleep, balanced mood, and sharp concentration.

3 Make your meals and snacks as complex as possible.

Our food comes from three major groups: carbohydrates, proteins, and fats. Fresh herbs and spices add another healthy dimension. To make meals and snacks complex, you simply need to **combine foods from different food groups.** This vastly increases the variety of nutrients you will eat and is a great way to keep your blood-sugar level naturally balanced.

CARBOHYDRATES: Whole grains such as oats, rye, wheat, spelt, barley, rice, corn, quinoa, buckwheat, and foods made from these, such as bread, pasta, and cereals; fruits and vegetables; honey, sugar, and syrup.

PROTEINS: Meat and poultry; fish; beans, pulses, and lentils; soy products; dairy products such as milk and cheese; eggs; nuts and seeds.

FATS: Meat and poultry, dairy foods; oils such as olive oil, flaxseed oil, coconut oil; nuts and seeds; oily fish, avocados, and olives.

Complex meals and snacks don't need to be time-consuming to prepare, they just need a bit more thought at the planning and organization stage.

★   An apple is a nutritious snack by itself, yet add a handful of nuts and it instantly becomes more complex—the apple provides carbohydrates and the nuts provide protein and fats, along with other essential vitamins and minerals.

★   A bowl of oatmeal made with milk is a nourishing breakfast. Adding some ground pumpkin and sunflower seeds, fresh berries, a spoonful of natural yogurt, and a dash of cinnamon increases both the complexity and health benefits.

★   Add protein-rich beans, lentils, or nuts and seeds to soups, salads, casseroles, and dips. This is an easy way to make meals and snacks instantly more complex.

4 Include color and variety in your daily diet.

If your daily diet includes a rainbow of colors, it will ensure that you are obtaining the widest possible range of nutrients from your food. Fruits and vegetables in particular come in a whole spectrum of different colors. If you **include a rich variety of natural colors in your diet**, every day becomes a visual feast for your senses and an excellent way to boost your health mindfully.

Variety isn't just limited to fruits and vegetables. As you know, humans can easily become creatures of habit, choosing the same foods day in, day out. It's no wonder people get bored and start to crave intensely sugary desserts and snacks—their taste buds are probably just crying out for something different. A good example is the vast amount of wheat-based products many people consume on a daily basis: cereal or toast for breakfast, a sandwich for lunch, pasta for dinner; add in a few cookies and cakes, and that's a dull, repetitive diet with a heavy bias toward wheat. The same is true for dairy products. You can choose instead to explore the rich variety of whole grains such as rye, oats, spelt, millet, corn, amaranth, buckwheat, quinoa, rice, and wheat. Try delicious dairy alternatives such as soy milk, almond milk, and nut butters. Adding variety to your daily diet makes it both more interesting and healthier than remaining stuck in a food rut.

5 Make friends with fat.

Fat has unfairly been blamed for many chronic health problems in Western society. Many people believe that all fat is bad and should be avoided as much as possible.

It's time to set the record straight. Just as you need a wide variety of colorful and complex carbohydrates and proteins in your diet, so, too, do you need a range of fats.

Many people are aware of the health problems associated with eating too many saturated fats, such as an increased risk of cardiovascular disease, yet most aren't aware that not eating enough beneficial fats can also cause health problems.

The following can be signs of a diet that is too low in beneficial fats:

* Dry, flaky skin

* Inflammation problems

* Dry eyes

* Hormone imbalances

* Mood fluctuations

* Poor memory and concentration

* Cardiovascular health problems

The simplest way to get your intake of fats back on track is to **include more beneficial unsaturated and polyunsaturated fats in your diet** and less saturated fats.

Foods high in saturated fats include red meat, butter, cheese, cream, cookies, pastries, and cakes. Try to cut down on these foods.

Mindfully eat more oily fish such as salmon, tuna, herring, anchovies, and mackerel (Please note, however, that there are concerns about the level of toxins in oily fish, so stick to just a couple of servings per week). Plain nuts, seeds, and their oils are also packed full of good fats.

6 Make plant-based foods the star attraction, rather than the supporting act.

It's a shame that legumes such as peas, beans, and lentils seem to have mysteriously vanished from Western diets. We believe it's time that these nutrient-dense, life-changing plant foods packed full of wholesome, health-giving properties made a comeback.

In 2004, best-selling author and explorer, Dan Buettner, teamed up with *National Geographic* and a group of longevity researchers to identify areas around the world where people lived significantly longer than average and with a measurably better quality of life. He named these areas the "Blue Zones" and went on to identify nine dietary and lifestyle characteristics common to the people living in these areas. For many of the people living in the Blue Zones, plant-based foods are the primary focus of their diets. This doesn't mean that they are strict vegetarians, but, rather, when meat is consumed it is considered a luxury and only the leanest, highest-quality cuts are chosen.

Colorful fruits, vegetables, and salads are powerhouses for your health. Peas, beans, and lentils are packed full of protein, fiber, vitamins, and minerals. Relatively inexpensive, they are simple to source and easy to cook with. There's something particularly mindful and wonderfully grounding about preparing and eating legumes. Perhaps it's the fact that they have been around for such a long time; beans have been grown in Thailand since approximately 7000 BCE and they even famously got a mention in Homer's *Iliad*.

To include more plant-based foods in your diet:

★ Try lots of varieties, such as garbanzo beans, red and green lentils, Puy lentils, haricot beans, edamame beans, cannellini beans, mung beans, kidney beans, black beans, pinto beans, adzuki beans, fava/broad beans, navy beans, lima beans, flageolet beans, and black-eyed peas.

★ You will easily find many different types of beans, pulses, and lentils in cans. Alternatively, you can buy dried versions, some of which will need to be soaked overnight before you can start cooking with them.

★ Peas, beans, and lentils work well in soups, salads, and casseroles. You can also turn them into delicious dips, spicy lentil dhals, and Moroccan inspired pâtés.

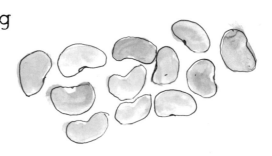

There is something mindful and wonderfully grounding about preparing and eating legumes.

7 Drink plenty of fresh, filtered water.

In terms of hydration, you simply can't beat water, yet caffeinated drinks such as tea and coffee, sugary sodas, and alcoholic drinks that dehydrate and disrupt blood-sugar balance are more often the norm. It's not unusual for people mindlessly to consume ten or more cups of coffee or tea daily. There is no need to avoid tea, coffee, and alcohol to live a healthy life; we simply encourage you to **be conscious of your drinking habits** to restore a healthy balance.

Water is essential. Without food, humans may survive for up to forty days but without water, we can only survive for around three days. Water transports essential nutrients and oxygen to cells, regulates temperature, and helps to flush out waste products. Up to 75 percent of your body is water, yet most people don't drink anywhere near enough on a daily basis.

We suggest that you start to **carry fresh, filtered water with you wherever you go,** and **listen to your body's own signals to decide when it's time to take another sip.** If you listen carefully, your body will tell you if you aren't drinking enough.

Tell-tale signs of thirst:

* Low energy

* Poor concentration

* Dry skin

* Dull hair

* Constipation

* Stiff joints

Thirst is often mistaken for hunger, so next time you're tempted to reach for an extra snack, sip a glass of water instead.

FOOD FOR THOUGHT

Being mindful helps you to see the extraordinary in something seemingly ordinary. Try this simple exercise with a glass of water and note your observations in your journal.

Prepare a fresh, cool glass of water, perhaps add a couple of ice cubes, a slice of fresh lemon or lime, and, finally, a fragrant sprig of freshly picked mint or rosemary. Put the glass down in front of you and consider how wonderful this clear liquid is, so critical for life, yet so often taken for granted. Marvel at the miracle of this elixir, upon which your life literally depends. Perhaps you will begin to see that water, something so seemingly ordinary, is in fact extraordinary? And, finally, ask yourself, how would you drink it if this were your last glass?

Take a sip. Savor. Enjoy.

Carry fresh, filtered water with you wherever you go.

8 Eat breakfast as soon as possible after you wake up.

In terms of health and well-being, breakfast is perhaps your most important meal of the day. Studies have shown that people who eat breakfast tend to be slimmer and find it easier to maintain a healthy weight than those who skip the first meal of the day.

The word "breakfast" has been used in the UK since the middle of the fifteenth century, and is likely to have been formed as a compound of two words, to represent breaking the overnight fast between dinner and the first meal of the day. Without breakfast, the fast continues, which makes it hard to get going in the morning. People often rely on quick-fix stimulants such as coffee instead. Without immediate access to food, your body may question whether there is a famine on the way, and, just in case there is, may slow everything down to preserve its valuable resources, leaving you feeling lethargic.

When you **choose to eat a wholesome breakfast** soon after you wake, your body can use this fuel to kick-start your energy for the day. You also send the message to your body that **there is more food on the way,** so it knows it is safe to fire on all cylinders, for optimum energy and performance.

When you make time for breakfast, you set a positive tone for your entire day. A rushed, stressful start often leads to a rushed, stressful day, whereas a mindful, relaxed, and nourished start will more likely be the start of a balanced day where you can take everything in your stride. A start like this will support balanced energy, mood, and concentration.

There are always many excuses not to start the day with a nutritious and mindful breakfast and having busy lives and families ourselves, we do understand this. However, after only a few days of getting up half an hour earlier, making time to **put this principle into practice**, you will be hooked, simply because you will feel so much better. **Take this one simple action** and it will have widespread effects not just on your eating habits but throughout your whole life.

AMELIE AND TOM'S SUPER SMOOTHIE

Great for a quick breakfast or nutritious snack, this smoothie is a firm favorite with children, especially ours! Experiment with a range of different ingredients so that your smoothie is different every time.

½ ripe banana or ½ ripe avocado

1 tbsp frozen berries (strawberries, raspberries, blackberries, blueberries)

or substitute for other frozen fruits to taste

Handful fresh spinach leaves

1 cup/250ml apple juice or almond milk (add more/less for a runnier/thicker consistency)

2 heaped tbsp live yoghurt or ¼ pack silken (smooth) tofu

1 tbsp ground sunflower seeds, pumpkin seeds, and linseeds

1 tsp chia seeds (you will find these in any good health food shop)

1 tbsp flaxseed oil

½ level tsp lecithin granules (you will find these in any good health food shop)

Serves 2

Liquidize all the ingredients to a smooth consistency and drink immediately.

Super Seed Mix

In a coffee grinder, grind ½ cup pumpkin seeds, ½ cup sunflower seeds, and ½ cup flaxseeds to a fine powder. Store in an airtight container in the fridge. Packed full of beneficial fats, you can add this seed mix to smoothies and salads, or use as a crunchy topping on steamed vegetables.

9 Plan your meals and snacks in advance, so that you can choose your food rather than it choosing you.

People who **maintain a healthy diet** are usually very organized in their approach to food.

When you plan what you are going to eat, not only will it help you to be in complete and conscious control of your food choices, food shopping will also become much easier and you will find that you spend and waste less too. Use your journal to make plans. Keep new recipes you want to try within easy reach. Choose to keep a stock of nutritious, portable snacks readily available. Make a fruit salad or a super salad in advance and store in the fridge so you can easily take a portion out and about with you. Take a packed lunch to work. Plan to succeed.

10 Allow yourself the foods you really love, in moderation.

This is one of the simplest but perhaps the most important of all the mindful principles. Healthy eating habits aren't about dieting and deprivation, instead, **they involve enjoyment of all aspects of food**, from growing and choosing, to preparing and cooking, and finally savoring the finished goods. Healthy food habits are balanced and **include all the foods you love**, so please do **allow yourself the foods you really enjoy**, in moderation. Move away from guilt and move towards mindful, balanced enjoyment.

FOOD FOR THOUGHT

It's time to put the mindful eating principles into practice.

In your journal, make a note of everything that you eat and drink over the next few days. Take some time to reflect on the food choices that you made with the new, mindful eating principles in mind.

Highlight the food choices that you made, which followed these principles. Using a different color, highlight those choices which are not in line with the principles and which you would like to change.

Are there certain times of the day, or particular situations when unwanted habits occur?

How can you incorporate some of the mindful eating principles into your daily life? Add color and variety to your diet, make meals and snacks more complex, and focus on whole foods that are cooked from scratch. Think about your water intake, consider making time for breakfast, and remember to eat regularly.

The final step is to put together a plan for a new day that is packed full of the mindful eating principles. This may be time-consuming at first, but with practice it will soon become second nature.

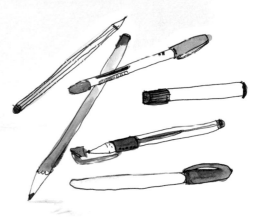

SPICED OATMEAL CAKE WITH CHOCOLATE AND CINNAMON FROSTING

Spend a lovely afternoon preparing and savoring this deliciously different cake, which is perfect for sharing with friends and family.

⅔ cup/80g rolled oats

1 stick/125g unsalted butter, at room temperature

½ cup/115g packed light soft brown sugar

½ cup/115g granulated/caster sugar

2 eggs

1⅓ cups/185g all-purpose/plain flour

1 tsp baking powder

1 tsp ground cinnamon

½ tsp freshly grated nutmeg

cinnamon chocolate frosting

¾ cup/200 ml light/single cream

6 oz/200g premium dark chocolate

½ tsp ground cinnamon

A springform cake pan, 8 inches/20 cm in diameter, lightly greased

and lined with baking paper

Serves 10–12

Preheat the oven to 350°F (180°C)/Gas 4.

Put the oats in a heatproof bowl. Add 1¼ cups/300ml boiling water and stir.

Cover with plastic wrap/clingfilm and let sit for 20 minutes.

Put the butter and both sugars in the mixing bowl and beat together until pale, thick,

and creamy.

Add one of the eggs and beat until well combined. Add the remaining egg and beat again. Stir in the flour, baking powder, cinnamon, and nutmeg, then fold in the softened oats. Spoon the mixture into the prepared cake pan and level the surface.

Bake in the preheated oven for 35–40 minutes, until golden. Let cool in the pan for 10 minutes, then transfer to a wire rack to cool completely.

To make the frosting, set a heatproof bowl over a saucepan of barely simmering water, making sure the boiling water does not come into contact with the bottom of the bowl. Pour the cream into the bowl and let it warm slightly. Add the chocolate and cinnamon and stir constantly until the chocolate has melted and the mixture is dark and smooth.

Remove from the heat and let cool for about 30 minutes, until the frosting has a thick, spreading consistency. Use a palette knife or spatula to spread the frosting evenly over the sides and top of the cake. Cut into slices to serve. The cake will keep in an airtight container for 2–3 days.

Chapter 6

Mindful Eating and Weight Loss

The Wise Chimp

There was once a wise chimp who lived with his community in the rainforest.

One day, he was sitting in a tree away from the group. A shot rang out and in shock he fell out of the tree and landed heavily on his leg, fracturing it in two places. He realized that this could well mark the end of life as he knew it. As he hung his head and worried he noticed a stick lying nearby. He picked it up and, over the coming days, he learned to walk with it, until he could eventually make his way back to the group. On his return, the younger chimps crowded around to hear his story. They were so taken by what he had learned that they began to imitate him and hobble around with stick crutches themselves.

Time passed. The wise chimp died and was forgotten, generations came and went, and the group continued to walk with crutches. They forgot how to live without them. One day, a chimp from far away approached the group and laughed at the chimps on crutches. They were understandably annoyed and dragged this upstart to the alpha male. The new chimp debated with the group for many hours, telling them how other chimps climbed trees freely without the aid of sticks. Some of the chimps began to believe him and agreed to let the new chimp help them. They set aside their crutches and began to take their first tentative steps alone. It was not easy for many of them at first.

Gradually, step by step, by following the new chimp and listening to their bodies for the first time, the vast majority progressed quickly and began to feel the benefits of a life unencumbered by their crutches. They were soon able to walk on their own two feet.

The Journey to a Healthy Weight

People are often motivated to change their eating habits because they are unhappy with their size and shape. Yet when you **start out on a journey towards a healthy weight it often leads to so much more**, as you find a multitude of additional benefits along the way.

If achieving a healthy weight is a specific goal for you, you will find that as you apply the nutrition principles from the previous chapter, **you are already well on your way toward your goal.**

Mindlessness allows you to stay in denial, unaware of your food habits and triggers, unconcerned with the benefits of food, and often concerned only with how to avoid food and consume as few calories as possible.

By shifting to a state of mindfulness, you **put yourself in the driver's seat** and **take full responsibility for where you are and where you want to be.** You learn to listen to your body and enjoy the process of eating real food. You consciously choose the food you want to eat for all the right reasons, rather than allowing it to unconsciously choose you. When **you are in this mindful state**, it becomes very difficult to overeat. As you are reading this, you may have started to notice that **this process is already well underway** for you. The work you have done so far has placed you **firmly on the right track**.

An understanding of food, health, and your body can help you to **become more mindful in your eating habits.** From a psychological perspective, if you understand why you are doing something, you are much more likely to **actually do it**. This way of thinking is particularly relevant for weight issues, where confusion reigns supreme. Most people we have worked with have tried many different diet plans and weight loss groups, and have also spent a lot of money on specialist "diet" food, yet they still find themselves a long way from their optimal weight. They instinctively know that something isn't working but struggle to know what that something is.

The generally accepted diet pattern is a vicious cycle of dieting and deprivation, followed by a period of overeating, then more dieting and deprivation, more overeating, and so on. Many people we meet have been on a diet for most of their lives and are left feeling fed up, depressed, and completely lacking in confidence, self-esteem, and the motivation to **do something about it**. Our message to them and to you is this: with the right support **you can change your eating habits for good**, without dieting or deprivation. You can **continue to eat the foods you love**, still **lose weight, and keep it off, for good**. Or, as one course participant said:

"I'm not on a diet. I have fundamentally changed the way I eat for good."

Andrew, 33

Achieving your healthy weight goal means engaging with food and your body at a deeper level.

We want you to become an expert on your body—no more confusion or fad diets, just good, honest, down-to-earth advice that makes sense, and works for you.

At its most basic level, body weight is just a case of simple math—calories in vs. calories out:

★ If you eat more calories than your body needs, your weight will increase.

★ If you eat fewer calories than your body needs, your weight will decrease.

★ If you match the calories you are eating with the calories you are using, your weight will stay the same.

Of course, the above is simply a guide and doesn't apply in all circumstances. These points assume that you are eating a well-balanced diet and that there are no underlying medical conditions that may make it difficult to maintain a healthy weight.

Fall In Love With Food, Forget Counting Calories

Although you do need to **get the balance right**, you can **leave calorie counting behind.** We want you to fall in love with real food. That doesn't involve looking at food and just seeing calories. Calorie counting can lead to an unhealthy relationship with food, as every meal or snack is judged on the number of calories it contains, rather than how beneficial it is for your health. It is difficult to enjoy a meal that has been meticulously weighed out and analyzed; food becomes functional and boring, and this is something you're likely to rebel against at a later stage.

When you are counting calories, it's all too easy to start viewing food as an enemy. It then becomes safer to stick to a routine of eating the same things, simply because you have no idea of how new foods will affect your weight. Aside from the nutritional deficits that occur when you eat the same foods day in, day out, it's also boring and unappealing, and so becomes unsustainable. You will crave something new, a break from the routine, and at some point you are likely to have an all-out binge on the foods you have been trying to avoid.

We encourage you to **change your eating habits for good.** We want you to get in tune with your mind and body, and mindfully **monitor your response to different foods**.

FOOD FOR THOUGHT

Make food your friend.

Imagine food as a person. Is it a friend or foe? What does this person look like? How do you feel about them? See the two of you together. What is your relationship like? Harmonious? Adversarial? Easy? Fraught? What do you think food feels like given these perceptions? (If they are not wholly positive at the moment, food may feel rejected, unloved, over-relied upon, undervalued, ignored). What kind of things would food like to say to you? Begin to communicate and hear its point of view. How would it like to be with you? How would you like to see food? How would you like your relationship to be from now on? Welcome food as a friend and start giving it the time, effort, respect, and love that you would give any good friend.

Just as with all people, there will be some aspects that you don't love as much as others, but since food is your friend, embrace it in all its wonder now.

CARROT AND LENTIL DIP

Prepare this nutritious dip in advance for a delicious portable snack or light lunch.

2 carrots, roughly chopped

1 red onion, chopped

1 garlic clove, chopped

1 tsp ground cumin

½ tsp ground coriander

½ tsp sea salt

3 tbsp olive oil

½ cup/120g dried red lentils

A handful of fresh cilantro/coriander leaves, finely chopped

Serves 6–8

Preheat the oven to 350°F (180°C)/Gas 4. Put the carrots, onion, garlic
cumin, ground coriander, salt, and 2 tablespoons of the oil in a bowl.
Toss and scatter the vegetables on a baking sheet. Cover with foil and cook
in the preheated oven for 45 minutes, until the carrots are just tender.
Increase the oven temperature to 425°F (220°C) Gas 7 and cook for a
further 10 minutes, until the carrots are golden. Let cool for 10 minutes.
Transfer to a food processor and process until chunky. Leave the mixture in
the food processor.
Cook the lentils in boiling water for 5 minutes, until just tender. Let sit in the
water for 10 minutes and then drain well.
Add the lentils to the carrot mixture and process until well combined.
Transfer to a serving bowl and stir in the remaining oil and the fresh
cilantro/coriander.
Serve with warmed flatbreads.

ROAST CINNAMON PLUMS
WITH PECAN NUTS

This simple combination makes a delicious dessert that is colorful, complex, and a visual delight.

¾ cup/175ml pineapple juice

1 tsp lemon juice

½ tsp ground cinnamon

2 cloves

1 star anise

1 tbsp pure organic maple or agave syrup

12 dark red plums, halved and pitted

A handful of pecan nut halves

1 cup/250ml thick plain (natural) bio yogurt

Serves 4

Preheat the oven to 400°F (200°C)/Gas 6. Mix together the pineapple and lemon juice, cinnamon, cloves, star anise, and maple or agave syrup in a large bowl. Add the plums and turn until coated in the mixture. Lift out the plums and reserve the juice. Arrange the plums, cut-side down, in a roasting pan. Bake for 30 minutes until slightly shriveled and softened. Put the pecan nuts on a baking sheet for 5 minutes until lightly golden. Remove the plums and pecan nuts from the oven.

Just before the plums are ready, put the pineapple juice mixture into a pan and bring to a boil. Turn down the heat and simmer for 5–8 minutes until thickened and syrupy. Remove the whole spices, then add the plums to the pineapple syrup.

Divide the plum mixture among four glasses. Top each serving with the yogurt. Roughly chop the pecan nuts and sprinkle over the yogurt before serving hot or cold.

Know Where You Are

The saying **"what gets measured gets done"** rings true for weight issues. When people don't keep track of where they're at, it's easy to ignore that the weight's creeping up and they keep it hidden in oversized baggy jumpers. When you chart your own progress regularly, you cannot stay in denial. There are a variety of ways you can **measure your progress**, we simply suggest that whatever you do, stick to it. Many course participants find it useful to create a graph to chart and record their weight at regular intervals; others prefer to use their clothes as a measure. One lady made a habit of trying on her "aspirational red dress" each morning to keep her on track. Choose a method that works for you and stick with it. When you are fully aware of where you are, **you make the minor daily adjustments necessary** in your eating to get where you want to be.

As you take steps to measure your own progress **you become the expert** in how you respond to different foods and ways of eating. We do not recommend a prescriptive diet plan; instead, we encourage you to **get to know your body inside and out** so that you know exactly how and when to adjust your food intake. This is essential for long-term success. When you keep a close eye on your own progress you will quickly notice when you're going off-track. You can then look back over your food diary and work out what went wrong, make any necessary adjustments, and move on. You may simply decide that you need to eat a little less or a little more overall. By closely tracking your own progress you will **become an expert on what suits you best**, and this will stay with you for the rest of your life.

Lose the Fat; Keep the Lean

There are many different tissues in the human body, including lean tissue and fat (adipose) tissue. When your weight changes, it means that you have either increased or decreased the amount of lean tissue, adipose tissue, or some of both. The most effective way to achieve a healthy weight is to target a reduction in fat stores. Unfortunately, many diet plans rely on severely reduced calories, fasting, and ravenous hunger to ensure rapid weight loss, which comes from lean tissue.

This lean tissue requires more calories to keep it going than fat tissue does. You may have heard people talk about having a "fast" or "slow" metabolism and this speed is directly related to how much lean tissue you have. The more lean tissue you have, the faster your metabolism will be, and you will burn off calories more quickly than someone who has less lean tissue. Having high levels of lean tissue is, therefore, a great help in both achieving and maintaining a healthy weight. Lean tissue is also packed full of helpful cells, which keep you well and promote healthy aging. You need to nurture these cells, not get rid of them. Aiming to reduce your fat stores will lead to healthy weight loss that can be maintained for good.

The mindful eating principles are specifically designed to support this healthy weight loss and balance your blood sugar level. Keeping blood sugar balanced is a key factor in healthy weight loss because when blood sugar is unbalanced, your body goes into "fat-storing" mode, which is exactly what you want to avoid. Eating regularly and avoiding ravenous hunger are also essential for encouraging your body to let go of unwanted fat stores. For healthy weight loss, you simply need to follow the principles outlined in chapter five, and be mindul of these additional suggestions that will help to propel you towards your goals:

Balance your grains—aim for one to two portions of "grain-type" carbohydrates daily (bread, pasta, rice, cereals, oatcakes, crackers, spelt, oats, couscous, buckwheat, and other grains.) One portion is equal to one slice of bread or a handful of cereal/cooked grains or equivalent. You can increase your intake of these foods when you have achieved your goals.

Balance your intake of denser/starchy grains—aim for one to two servings per day of vegetables such as potatoes, sweet potatoes, carrots, turnips, parsnips, squash, and beetroot. One serving is equal to half a sweet potato or equivalent. We encourage you to eat a wide range of all other vegetables daily and to prioritize vegetables over fruit.

Aim for a steady weight loss—1–2 lbs per week is ideal. Steady weight loss is key for targeting fat stores and will ensure that you can maintain the weight loss for good.

Track your progress—this will allow you to know when to adjust your intake of the aforementioned foods in particular.

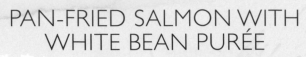

PAN-FRIED SALMON WITH WHITE BEAN PURÉE

Using beans instead of rice, potatoes, or pasta is a great way to approach many dishes when you are cutting down on grain-type carbohydrates and working towards your healthy weight goals.

2½oz/65g arugula/rocket leaves

3½oz/90g baby spinach leaves

2oz/50g watercress or more arugula leaves

16 cherry tomatoes, halved

1 tbsp olive oil

4 garlic cloves, halved

4 salmon fillets, about 6½oz/185g each, trimmed and bones removed

Balsamic vinegar, for drizzling

Extra-virgin olive oil, for drizzling

Sea salt and ground black pepper

White Bean Purée

14oz/400g can cannellini beans, rinsed and drained

1 garlic clove, crushed

1½ tbsp lemon juice

2 tbsp chopped fresh thyme

2 tsp olive oil

Serves 4

Reserve a few arugula leaves for serving, then put the remaining arugula, spinach, and watercress, if using, in a salad bowl. Add the cherry tomatoes and set aside.

To make the white bean purée, put the beans, garlic, lemon juice, thyme, oil, and 2 tbsp of water in a food processor or blender. Season with salt and pepper to taste, then process to a smooth, soft, purée. Add a little more water if necessary. Transfer to a pan and heat gently for about 5 minutes, stirring frequently, until piping hot. (Alternatively, put the purée in a microwaveable bowl, cover, and cook on high for about 4 minutes, stirring halfway through, until piping hot. Let stand for 1 minute before serving.)

Meanwhile, to cook the salmon fillets, heat the oil in a nonstick sauté pan. Add the garlic and fry gently for 1 minute. Add the salmon and cook for 5–8 minutes, turning once halfway through.

Drizzle the salad with a little balsamic vinegar, season to taste with salt and pepper, and toss well. Put a spoonful of white bean purée onto each of four warmed serving plates. Put the reserved arugula leaves on top, followed by the salmon. Drizzle with a little olive oil. Serve immediately with the salad.

Relax

When the body is under stress, blood sugar levels become unbalanced and, as a result, the body goes into fat-storing mode. Simply doing something to help you de-stress is the key—when you **decide to take even the smallest action to deal with stress** you send the message to your unconscious that **you are in charge and you can do it differently.** Having mindful eating habits and making time for relaxed meals is a great thing to do, as is fostering the healthy habit of regularly getting a good night's sleep.

Take action to deal with stress.

You are in charge and can do it differently.

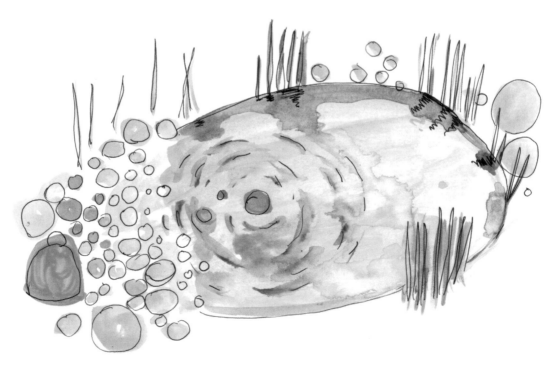

FOOD FOR THOUGHT

The following sensory exercises will help you to de-stress. Try them all and find the one that nurtures you the most.

Sound: play music—any variety that changes your state.

Sight: look at a beautiful scene or object, which encourages the mindful state you want to achieve. This could be a candle, a flower, or your dog. If it helps you, make a scrapbook of calming pictures or put them on your desktop. Shut your eyes and keep the pictures in your mind.

Inner monologue: interrupt your repetitive self-talk by listening to something positive, such as a motivational speaker (we love TED talks), or a guided meditation. The key is to reframe any stress so that you feel better about it.

Feeling: Exercise is a fabulous state changer, but another option could be EFT (Emotional Freedom Technique). One such technique is to tap on different energy points where meridians cross in the body.

Here is a quick version:

Rate your level of stress one a scale of one to ten (ten is the highest).

Hold the stress in your mind—focus on it while you tap firmly but gently on the following points with your knuckles:

The side of your hand.

The collarbone (the point at which the knot of a tie would sit).

The crown of the head.

Tap on each point for a few seconds and then rate your stress level again—how much has it gone down? Repeat until you feel your stress has significantly decreased. Make sure you hold the stress feelings in mind as you do this. Which of the points changes your state the most? Combine more than one and see which are the most helpful.

Food, Mood, and Weight Loss

"Everything we do is either an act of love or a cry for help."

Marianne Williamson

For many people, food cravings can get in the way of putting mindful eating into practice. Some cravings are physiological, such as the intense craving you get when your blood sugar is out of balance. You can proactively deal with these types of cravings by naturally managing your own diet.

Many cravings, however, are psychological. People often eat for reasons such as stress, anger, or sadness. Just as you can proactively manage your blood sugar, you can **be proactive about psychological cravings** by learning to listen to them, and discovering what it is they're really asking you for.

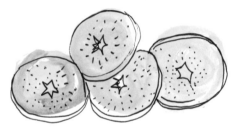

Eating For Comfort

Eating and comfort are associated from birth (and before). Feeding is at the core of the bond between mother and child. When you cried as a baby, your mother's first reaction would often have been to feed you. This taught you to equate food not just with nourishment, but with safety, peace of mind, and, most importantly, with love. When you hurt yourself and cried as an older child, your carers may have given you something sweet to pacify you. Putting something in your mouth literally stops the cries, and the same is true of an adult trying to push down their emotions with food.

The equation that "food = love" often continues throughout our lives. Perhaps your parents or guardians rewarded you with sweet treats for good behavior, or removed sweets as a punishment. Maybe they found it easier to show love by feeding you than by being demonstrative with hugs and reassurances. Perhaps you saw adults using food as a replacement for love when they were upset or angry. In many cultures feeding people is a practical way to show you care. Food and comfort can get so mixed up in the brain that food often becomes a substitute for the love that you really want.

How do you spot emotional hunger? Let's start to separate genuine physical hunger from cravings that are not really about food at all.

There are three important characteristics of emotional hunger.

1 The context: when it happens and with whom.

Do you find yourself at the cookie jar every time you hang up the phone after talking to a particular relative or work colleague, when your child plays up, or when something goes wrong at work? If so, this is emotional rather than physical hunger.

2 The substance: what you crave.

There are very few people in the world who comfort-eat broccoli or celery. People tend to crave carbohydrates and sugar for comfort. If you're physically hungry, carrots will look as good as cake. If you're emotionally hungry, only your preferred fix will do.

3 How it happens: the timing

Physical hunger builds over time whereas cravings develop quickly and nag at you persistently. Teach yourself to **become aware of the emotions that trigger your cravings**. Mindfully stay with the craving, listen to the message it has for you, and then do something to make yourself feel better that doesn't involve using less than healthy food as a substitute.

Your Favorite Fixes

What foods do you crave? What is it you are most likely to reach for? People usually crave foods like chocolate, wine, cake, cookies, or pasta. The foods you crave are probably the foods you have a love–hate relationship with. You eat them, but you don't like that you eat them. The trouble is that the more you resist the craving, the more it will persist.

The first thing you can do is to **be prepared to sit with it**. The simple act of focusing on the feeling begins to change it. Cravings, just like any other strong feeling, do not last long if you **simply let them play out**.

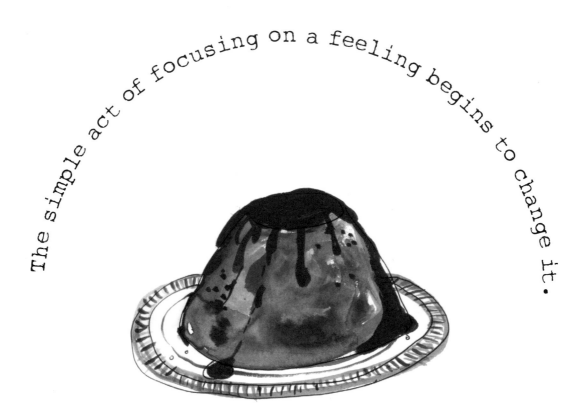

The simple act of focusing on a feeling begins to change it.

FOOD FOR THOUGHT

*"Do you have the patience to wait
Till the mud settles and the water is clear?
Can you remain unmoving
Till the right action arises by itself?"*

Lao-Tzu

Make peace with the food you crave.

Sit with the food you crave and observe it. See yourself watching the food and observe your own reactions to it. Really be there with any feelings and observe whatever comes. Steer clear of judgment and put your focus on letting go of any disapproval. Be curious. Give yourself full permission to eat it here and now, if that's what you would like to do. Eat it as slowly and mindfully as you can, paying close attention to the texture, smell, and taste, and focus on what you feel as you eat it. Let go of any negative feelings or judgments. Release any disapproval with every breath, then begin to breathe in acceptance for yourself and for the food. Accept the food for what it really is—it's just foodstuff. Judgment blocks, love transforms.

Satisfy Your Craving Without Food

Any kind of strong craving is your body telling you that there is something out of balance, and if you are prepared to listen to it you will **discover the message that it has for you.** If you've ever tried to keep a small child quiet while you are on the phone you'll know that the more you push them away or ignore them, the louder they get. Similarly, if you continually ignore the body's message, it will shout louder and louder until you listen. So **attend to the part of you that is trying to communicate.** When you understand what the real intention of your craving is, you can find ways to satisfy it without food.

Once you know what the craving is about emotionally, you need to find a way to satisfy it without food. For example, if what you are seeking is love, go get a hug. If you need peace, go and meditate, get some fresh air, or listen to your favorite music. Do something that truly nurtures you. If you can't do it right now, do something to shift the emotion until you are able to get the thing that you truly crave.

Looking after yourself is the best treat you can give to your body and spirit. Many people spend their lives looking after others but neglect their own well-being. On a plane, the safety advice is: "make sure you put on your own oxygen mask before you help anyone else with theirs." You have to **be self-interested** in order to be selfless. You have to **put yourself first** if you want to **be of use to other people.**

Emotional hunger is often simply an indication that your reserves of self-nurture are running low and you need to take care of yourself. If you do what most people do and beat yourself with a metaphorical stick whenever you reach for a cookie, you won't actually change anything. Talk to yourself like you would talk to your best friend (rather than an enemy) and treat yourself well.

SPICY PINTO BEAN SOUP WITH SHREDDED LETTUCE AND NATURAL YOGURT

Take your time over this hearty soup and savor its different flavors, textures, and temperatures. Enjoy it on its own, or with a colorful super salad.

½ cup/100g dried pinto beans

2 tbsp butter

1 tbsp olive oil

1 red onion, chopped

2 garlic cloves, chopped

1 red bell pepper, deseeded and diced

2 carrots, chopped

2 tsp chili powder

2 tsp ground cumin

2 bay leaves

6 cups/1.5 liters vegetable stock

14oz/400g can chopped tomatoes

Sea salt

To serve

1 small iceberg lettuce, finely shredded

Natural yogurt

Leaves from a small bunch of fresh

cilantro/coriander

Lime wedges

Serves 4

Soak the beans in cold water overnight. Drain and set aside.

Heat the butter and oil in a large, heavy-based saucepan set over medium heat. Add the onion, garlic, red pepper, and carrots along with a pinch of salt. Cook for 10 minutes, until softened. Stir in the chili powder, cumin, and bay leaves, and cook for 1 minute, until aromatic. Increase the heat to high. Add the stock, tomatoes, and beans, and bring to the boil. Reduce the heat to a medium simmer and cook, uncovered, for about 45 minutes, until the beans are tender. Serve topped with shredded lettuce, a dollop of natural yogurt, and a few cilantro/coriander leaves. Offer lime wedges on the side for squeezing.

Take the Weight Off

Imagine that you're on a journey, walking along a path in a beautiful natural setting. Notice your surroundings and what your path is like. Does it twist and turn or is it straight? Is it bumpy or smooth? Perhaps you'll particularly enjoy the contrasting shades of colors, or be aware of the tall trees, the sky, or the clouds. Many people enjoy the sounds of nature, like the wind in the trees, a nearby stream, or birds singing. Perhaps you'll notice the warmth of the sun against your skin, or the texture of things you touch along the way.

Imagine that you're carrying a large backpack filled with stones, which you've had for quite a while. Feel the burden of the backpack, and notice that the extra weight makes movement more difficult and hampers your enjoyment. Imagine that each stone has been infused with a particular stress or worry in your life. Each time you reach an incline in the path and you are walking uphill the pack feels heavy, and you are looking forward to when you can drop the weight and leave those heavy thoughts behind.

Notice that up ahead of you the path leads to a derelict house; imagine that this is there for you to restore. Look at the details of the house as you approach, its design, what it's made from, its size, and particularly the garden. Begin to visualize what you would like to do to make it into a beautiful tranquil space.

Find a place to sit and take off that heavy backpack. Are you tired of carrying that heavy burden of stress around in your life? Perhaps it's time to leave it behind for good? Open the pack and take a closer look at those stones, each infused with the different stressors that have been weighing you down. What do they look like? Examine them closely and ask yourself what they represent for you now. Rather than throwing these rocks away, we are going to put them to good use as the foundation for your garden, to remind you of where you've come from and what you want to build for the future. Find a place for the rocks in the garden; you may want to build a bench from them, a pond, a wall, or bury them as the base of a flowerbed. Now take them out of the backpack one by one and build your chosen feature.

With every stone you shed, allow yourself to feel lighter. Every time you drop a stone, feel the sense of enjoyment that comes from taking positive action to construct your ideal future. By the time the last stone is gone from your backpack, you can allow yourself to feel a real sense of accomplishment that comes from a job well done.

Take positive action to construct your ideal future.

Chapter 7

Mindful Eating for Life

Plan for Success

There was once a young Italian man named Luigi who lived in a grand family home with a courtyard. In that courtyard was a garden filled with fragrant flowers and plants, but what it had in color it lacked in shade. One day, Luigi came home from lunch and found his 90-year-old uncle in the garden. He was working up a sweat, digging hole after hole to plant seedlings in the ground. Luigi approached him and said: "Uncle, what are you doing?"

"I am planting mango trees, my boy," he said with a smile.

"But why, uncle?" asked Luigi.

"Isn't it obvious? When these trees grow they will be beautiful. Imagine the fruit they will bear and the shade they will provide. This garden will be even more wonderful."

"Hmmm," said the boy, "but you are 90 years old and it takes at least 10 years for mango trees to bear fruit. Why would you go to all this trouble when you may not even be here to see the tree bear fruit?"

"Of course I won't be here. I'm not planting these mango trees for me. For 90 years, I've eaten fruit from trees planted by others and before I go I want to give back by planting as many trees as I can. Now leave me boy, time is short."

The Power of Belief

"If you believe you can or you can't, either way you are right."

Henry Ford

As you make changes to your way of eating, you might notice some resistance to change that can emerge in the form of excuses for not sticking to your plans. These surface spontaneously in the moment as a form of self-sabotage. Favorite excuses usually center around time, money, and energy:

"I can't do this now because I don't have time."

"This might work for other people but not for me."

"I don't have the willpower, so I can't stick to the program."

"Eating healthily is too expensive."

Although your excuses will let you off the hook in the moment, they will gradually undermine you over time. If you tell yourself something often enough, you will start to believe it. If you say "I can't find time to eat well" on a regular basis, it will become real for you, and it will sabotage your capacity to live the life you want.

Your **beliefs color your experience**, thereby shaping your reality. We all see and experience a different reality based on our beliefs about the world. If you believe you can't do something, this all too easily becomes a self-fulfilling prophecy. Think about the implications of this in your reality and how it might have an impact on you trying to improve your eating habits. For example, if you believe you can't **make time for eating mindfully** you will eventually prove yourself right: even if you manage to **fit in a mindful breakfast** four days this week, your focus will be on the days when you failed to have breakfast. Also, if you believe you've no time to eat mindfully now, the likelihood is you won't even try.

FOOD FOR THOUGHT

What are you saying to yourself about food and your capacity to change the way you eat? How will these thoughts determine your success? Negative internal thoughts become limiting beliefs.

Ask yourself: "On a scale of one to ten, how much do I actually believe I can make the long-term changes necessary to reach my goals?" If the answer is less than nine, it's likely you may have limiting beliefs that are getting in the way. This means you are likely to self-sabotage.

Limiting beliefs are often in the form of "I can't," "I won't," or "I should." The following list contains some common ones. Read the list out loud, slowly and mindfully, tune in to yourself, and feel your response. If a statement feels true for you, maybe it's something you can re-consider? Which of your limiting beliefs could you let go of right now?

· I can't enjoy myself without wine/coffee/cake.

· I can't change in the long term—I can change in the short term but then I revert to type.

· I can't ever be slim because of my genes.

· I won't feel happy without the reward that food gives me.

· I won't be taken seriously.

· I should eat everything on my plate.

Imagine your beliefs as layers of an onion that you can peel away piece by piece to find the real you. This is known as the "neti neti" process (meaning "neither this, nor that") in Eastern philosophy. Each layer could be a different belief you have about food. As soon as you begin to observe them, you will notice that they are not an essential part of you because you are the observer, not the observed.

Strip off some layers of your onion and observe them. Only keep the ones that serve you.

Your Beliefs Aren't Your Own

Best-selling author Alan Cohen said: **"Our history is not our destiny."** Your future is not limited by your past beliefs, unless you let it be. You may have lived with some beliefs from the age of six, but now it is time to question them.

You can choose new, empowering beliefs that support your goals, but first you must **let go of the old beliefs** that are sabotaging you. The first step to letting go of outdated beliefs is to **know that many of these beliefs are not originally your own.** Where did these limiting beliefs come from?

As a child, you start out as a shiny, clear point of consciousness—the epitome of mindfulness—living in the moment and soaking up every experience, just like a sponge. Children inherit their parents' beliefs about what's possible. As a five-year-old you didn't critically evaluate the words and actions of your parents or teachers to filter out what was not true. You just digested them whole as "reality." If one parent was constantly on a diet, you saw that as the thing to do; if the other parent avoided butter and chose low-fat food products, you believed that was the way to eat healthily. You believed your father completely when he said: "Everyone in our family is overweight. It's in our genes." Once you have a belief, you then go out into the world and find evidence to prove it, until your belief is so deeply ingrained that you forget that it is just a belief and you start to call it reality.

Let go of old beliefs.

Choose new, empowering beliefs.

Spring-Clean Your Beliefs

If you want to **make space for new and useful ideas and practices in your life**, you need to spring-clean your mind regularly, just as you would your home. You can **filter your beliefs** in order to **decide which ones still serve you** and which you would be happy to throw out. You've already begun this process of de-cluttering your belief system by examining your own set of disempowering food-related beliefs. Now it's time to bag them up and recycle them into something more useful.

You have changed many beliefs in your time. Beliefs about the nature of the world have also radically changed over time. People used to believe that the sun orbited the Earth and that the Earth was flat. Just as scientists need to keep an open mind in order to come closer to discovering the true nature of reality, you need to **keep an open mind** about your own experiences and regularly audit your beliefs. When you find out that you don't know something you thought you knew for sure, you **open the doors to greater learning**.

Plant New Beliefs

*"The best time to plant a tree is twenty years ago.
The second best time is now."*

Chinese Proverb

At the start of this program we asked you to **throw out your junk food and prepare your cupboards** for your new, thoughtfully chosen food. We are now asking you to throw out your outmoded beliefs and **make space for the new** ones that are more suited to who you are now and who you want to be.

Start to **assert your new belief** and then **look for evidence to back it up.** If you start to tell yourself that you can find time for breakfast, prepare lunch in advance, or **be excited about eating nutritious food,** your mind will start to search for reasons to support these beliefs. If you start to entertain the "I can" possibility, the creative part of your brain will start to **find new, innovative solutions** to put these beliefs into practice.

Act now to change some of your negatives into positives. Write them down in your journal and look at them frequently. Now, still yourself and run through your memories to find evidence in your life for this new belief. Research it and read stories about people who have that belief. Even better, go and seek out an experience that will back up your new belief right now. Make it a priority to reinforce it constantly.

Allow New Beliefs to Take Root

"Your beliefs become your thoughts,
Your thoughts become your words,
Your words become your actions,
Your actions become your habits,
Your habits become your values,
Your values become your destiny."

Mahatma Gandhi

If **you can change your beliefs you can change your world**. Buddha described the mind as being full of drunken monkeys who jumped, screeched, and chatted endlessly. Negative thoughts tend to be especially loud monkeys. Buddha taught meditation as a way to tame the drunken monkeys in the mind, and the following suggestion will help you to work mindfully with your beliefs as soon as they pop into your mind as thoughts.

✳ Stop yourself in your tracks each time you want to say something negative to yourself. A mindful way to interrupt negative thoughts is to begin counting up from one each time a negative thought comes to mind. As soon as another thought pops in, start your counting from one again. When you do this at first, you may find you can only get to four or five before you need to begin again, but you will gradually extend the time you can remain free from negative thoughts. Once the thoughts have gone, mindfully focus on what you do want to believe instead. Hold the positive belief in your mind for as long as you can. When your awareness shifts, gently bring it back to the belief you want. When you finish, immediately cement this for yourself with action, based on your new belief. Eat a soup and a salad, cook a delicious mindful recipe, eat something different for breakfast, or take ages over lunch.

Make Mindful Eating Part of Daily Life

Change often requires re-organization. You have been working on yourself to develop new positive habits, beliefs, and actions. To ensure that these changes take permanent root, you need to consider how you can make mindful eating fit into your daily life.

Did you know that if a number of crabs are trapped in a bucket and one manages to escape, the other crabs would invariably try to pull it back in? Similarly, people naturally tend to resist change at first, even if that **change is for the better,** because the old way is familiar, safe, and easy. The people around you might try to pull you back in subtle ways, for example, by tempting you with unhealthy foods. You might also sabotage yourself by beginning to allow the excuses to creep back in. **Success happens when you have the courage to stand up for what you believe in** and **keep going in the face of resistance**.

It might be easier to continue overeating because mindful eating initially takes time, planning, energy, and plenty more of your resources. Know now that **you have all the resources you need to succeed** inside you, and that it's always worth it in the end.

Find Your Mindful Tribe

We have found that something wonderful can happen when two or more people **come together to work towards a common goal.** The creative and thoughtful ways that people find to support one another never cease to amaze and inspire us. Daily encouraging emails and texts, group soup-swaps, walk and talk meet-ups, traditional bread-making afternoons, group-meditation workshops, and even creative evenings spent writing in journals have all been woven into group support. You will find that when you **nourish yourself with mindful food**, you will start to nurture yourself in other areas of your life too.

Maybe you can work through the mindful eating program with a group of friends. **Plan specific times for support,** schedule regular meet-ups in your diaries, and stick to them. Keep things interesting and change the location of your meetings regularly. If you normally meet in a coffee shop, why not go for a walk instead, and chat along the way? Take a flask of freshly made mint tea and some mindful nibbles, or plan a picnic.

People are often more inclined to look for support when they're struggling, but **your support network will work best when you fully commit and get involved**, especially when you're riding the crest of the wave. **Celebrate all your successes with your mindful tribe**, no matter how small. Change is contagious and you will find that your successes will magically weave their way through the rest of your group.

A MINDFUL PICNIC

Who can resist the sight of a wicker hamper topped with a folded woolen blanket, waiting at the door, ready for an afternoon outdoors? Take your time to plan a mindful picnic and fill your hamper with delicious mindful goodness. Pick your destination and then spend the afternoon savoring every single taste. Make daisy chains. Cloud watch. Daydream.

FRESH VIRGIN MARY

Hint: Freeze in a plastic container in advance and it will be deliciously cool by the time you arrive, as it will have slightly defrosted.

6 ripe tomatoes

3 celery sticks

1 garlic clove (optional)

1 red chili, seeded

Ice cubes

A large pinch of celery salt (optional)

Serves 1

To skin the tomatoes, cut a small cross in the base, put into a large bowl, and cover with boiling water. Leave for 1 minute, then drain and pull off the skins.
Juice the tomatoes, celery, garlic (if using), and chili. Pour into a jug of ice, stir in the celery salt (if using) then serve.

ITALIAN LENTIL SALAD

2 cups/150g cooked or canned brown lentils, rinsed and drained (1 cup/225g raw weight)

4 preserved baby artichokes, preferably broiled (grilled), quartered

1 red onion, halved lengthways and cut into thin wedges

1½ cups/175g diced, or roughly crumbled feta cheese

A handful of mixed fresh herbs, such as parsley, basil, or marjoram, coarsely chopped, or chopped chives, plus herb sprigs to garnish

ITALIAN DRESSING

1 tbsp cider vinegar

¼ cup/60 ml extra-virgin olive oil

Ground black pepper

A pinch of sea salt, if needed

Serves 4

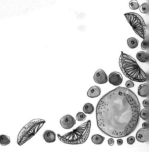

Put the lentils in a bowl and add the vinegar, oil, and pepper.

Add the artichokes, onion, and feta cheese, then toss together gently. Add salt and pepper to taste—remember that the feta cheese is already salty. Serve sprinkled with the mixed herbs and garnished with an herb sprig.

FIG, ALMOND, AND RAW CACAO BARS

½ cup/50g hazelnuts

½ cup/50g blanched almonds

½ cup/75g whole rolled oats (porridge oats)

Generous 1 cup/100g ready-to-eat dried figs, cut into small pieces

1¼ cups/150g unsulfured ready-to-eat dried apricots, cut into small pieces

2 tbsp raw cacao powder

5 tbsp fresh orange juice

2 tbsp dry unsweetened shredded (desiccated) coconut

Makes 12

Heat the oven to 350°F (180°C)/Gas 4. Put the hazelnuts and almonds on a baking sheet and roast for 6–8 minutes, turning once, until lightly golden. While the nuts are roasting, put the oats on a baking sheet and bake for 5 minutes until beginning to change color. Leave the nuts and oats to cool.

Put the nuts and oats in a food processor and process until finely chopped, then tip into a large bowl.

Put the figs, apricots, cacao powder, and orange juice into the processor and blend to a thick purée. Spoon the puréed fruit and coconut into the bowl with the oat mixture. Stir until combined into a thick paste, adding more cacao powder if too wet.

Line a 10 x 7in/25 x 18cm shallow pan (tin) with baking paper. Tip the fruit mixture into the pan and, using a wet metal spatula, spread into an even layer, about ½in/1cm thick. Chill in the refrigerator for about 1 hour to firm up.

Cut into bars and store in an airtight container in the refrigerator for up to one week.

FALAFEL WITH MINTED YOGURT

¾ cup/150g dried fava/broad beans,
preferably peeled

1 cup/220g dried chickpeas

1 large onion, chopped

8 garlic cloves, chopped

A small bunch of fresh flat leaf parsley,
chopped

Leaves from a bunch of fresh
cilantro/coriander, chopped

1 tbsp ground cumin

2 tsp ground coriander

¼ tsp chili powder

2 tsp sea salt

Vegetable oil, for shallow frying

Minted Yogurt

1 cup/250ml Greek-style yogurt

2 garlic cloves, crushed

A handful of fresh mint leaves, finely chopped

Makes about 30

Soak the fava/broad beans in cold water for 24 hours. Soak the chickpeas in cold water for at least 12 hours or overnight. If using unpeeled fava/broad beans you will need to rub the skins off and discard them.

Put the fava/broad beans in a food processor and process until fine and crumbly. Transfer to a large bowl. Do the same with the chickpeas, putting them in the bowl with the fava/broad beans.

Put the onion, garlic, parsley, and fresh cilantro/coriander in a food processor and process until well-combined. Add this mixture to the beans with the cumin, ground cilantro/coriander, chili powder, and salt. Use a large spoon to combine the mixture. Set aside and let sit for 30 minutes.

Pour sufficient oil in a frying pan to come about 1in/2.5cm up the side and heat over low/medium heat. The oil is ready when the surface is shimmering and a pinch of the mixture sizzles on contact with the oil. Using two dessertspoons, form the mixture into oval patties. Drop directly into the hot oil and cook for 2–3 minutes, turning halfway through until golden and crispy. Transfer to a plate lined with paper towels.

To make the minted yogurt, put the yogurt, garlic, and mint in a bowl and stir well to combine. Dip the falafel into the minted yogurt and enjoy.

FOOD FOR THOUGHT

Surround yourself with great role models. What messages are you getting in your current environment from the people you see, the things you read, watch, and talk about with your friends? Are they empowering? Do they support your growth? What messages do they give you about life? Do they match what you want to see in your life? Some television shows, for example, are a catalogue of disasters. Take an inventory and only give time to those things that reinforce your new positive lifestyle. Surround yourself with people who support you and your positive beliefs about yourself. Read books by people who've done what you want to do. Listen to uplifting broadcasts. Meditate each morning. Find your mindful tribe.

Choose role models who support you and your positive beliefs.

Make Time for Mindful Eating

The "I don't have time" excuse is a common one. We are fully aware of the challenges of putting these ideas into practice, especially when time already seems stretched. You can't **manufacture more time**, but what you can do is **make the most of the time you do have**. The key to success here centers around two key points:

1 Make it a priority to spend time nurturing the things that are most important in helping you reach your goals.

We have seen people swap half an hour of watching television for half an hour of making a mindful bean soup instead. Some people have ditched their daily wind-down with wine and chocolate and have replaced this with a family walk. Make sure that you regularly revisit your goals to ensure that you are spending your time nurturing the things that are most important to you.

2 Get organized.

We have found that when you **make time to be more mindful** this actually frees up more time. When you are mindful, your focus sharpens and you will **become more efficient at everything you do**. You will also start to filter out daily tasks and activities that are not helpful and don't fit with your new healthy lifestyle. Once you've identified what's important to you, you will **find the time to put your new way of eating into practice**.

Plan for Setbacks

"Failure is simply the opportunity to begin again,
this time more intelligently."

Henry Ford

Problems present opportunities to grow and change. Just as pearls are formed from grit, strength comes from overcoming life's issues. People make mistakes, and when you are learning to practice mindfulness in your eating you will occasionally encounter setbacks. **Keep going even when you have setbacks**—in fact, plan for these times. Imagine a time when you have some fast food, eat mindlessly, or eat because you feel sad. See yourself getting back up again, dusting yourself off, and continuing on your mindful path. Imagine this happening several times, and then see yourself looking back and laughing at your mistakes. Know that each setback taught you something that will help you become the person you want to be. There is no failure here, only learning. Welcome mistakes because they are how we learn. **Take it easy on yourself**; when you make a mistake that's the time when you are most in need of kindness. Reassure yourself this is just a blip and you are still learning.

Mindful Eating at Work

Being organized is key to your success in practicing mindful eating at work. You may **choose to keep a healthy supply of nuts and seeds on your desk**; one **simple change can make a big difference**. Your mindful eating program may also have positive effects on those around you. Work colleagues become curious, at first resisting and questioning these new habits, but then usually joining in once they see you blossom. Some people on the program have worried about long meetings where coffee, cookies, and chips were the only refreshments on offer. However, they soon found that being mindful quickly gave them newfound focus, heightened awareness, and higher self-esteem. They had compelling goals to work toward and found it easy to put themselves first and resist self-sabotaging by bringing their own healthy snacks to work meetings.

Eating Mindfully with Your Family

The stories we've been privileged to hear about the effects of mindful eating on the family unit are always incredibly touching. Slowing down and enjoying meals together as a family is one of the few precious moments when you **come together to share your experiences of the day**. For many, though, this time has been lost. When you **mindfully share a meal as a family**, you **strengthen your relationships**, solve your problems, and make lasting memories. Food can uniquely **bind your family together**. What a wonderful lasting gift to give to your children as they grow up, surrounded by a healthy, mindful relationship with good food.

If you have children, why not get them involved in growing, preparing, and cooking food? Go grocery shopping together and let them pick out unusual produce. Let older children plan and cook dinner for you, from start to finish. Have date nights with your partner where you spoil each other with a candlelit home-cooked meal that you have planned and prepared together. By involving your family in all aspects of food, from shopping to preparation, and finally enjoying it together, you will sow mindful seeds that will flourish for many years to come.

Make One Change

"Though no one can go back and make a brand new start, anyone can start from now and make a brand new ending."

Carl Bard

You may be ready to **work through every aspect of the program** and **give your eating habits a complete overhaul** straight away, or you may decide to just change one thing to start with. Do tell yourself that whatever you can do right now is right for you in this time and place, and is absolutely worth it. Know, too, that sometimes it's the smallest change that makes the biggest difference to your life. We encourage you to give your full attention to the changes you make, no matter how small. For example, you will experience many health and well-being benefits just from the simple act of making time for a mindful breakfast. This may seem like a small change, yet over the course of a year, that's 365 mindful breakfasts that you've made time for. If you don't currently eat together as a family or with your partner, can you **start by sharing just one meal together each day**? You will see benefits of these small changes accrue over time. You don't need to change everything at once, you just need to **get started and do something**.

How Will Your Garden Grow?

Consider for a moment what's involved in growing plants in a garden. Often, before you can start, the soil needs a bit of attention. You might need to pull out a few weeds and clear away anything else that could get in your way. It might also be a while before you get to the point where you clear out all the old stuff completely and you can start to plant something new and better.

You start by doing what you can: the work it takes to clear away, get rid of the rubble, pull up the weeds, dig up the roots, and so on. Then it's time to add some fresh, new nutrient-rich soil and mix it in, break up the old soil, and make sure it's nice and refreshed. Next, it's time to irrigate it. The soil needs plenty of water to refresh it and allow for new growth. While you are doing the preparation, you can take time to plan what you want to see growing there, and gather together your chosen seeds and seedlings. Finally, it's time to plant the seeds. This is the truly delightful part; planting seeds and enjoying thinking about how they will look when they grow, knowing that they will turn into wonderful things for the future.

Once you've planted your seeds it's time to take a short break. For the next week or two, occasionally you'll need to come back and water them, but the thing about planting seeds is that you have to give them time to grow. The best you can do is go away for a while and come back after you've done something else that's more productive. You can notice the weeds growing, but it won't hurt to let them go a bit before pulling them out. Occasionally you might need to add some water, but the sun and the rain will also take care of the process.

After the seeds have had time to start growing, it's time to begin regular maintenance. You water the seedlings and begin pulling the weeds. The first time you do this, it might be tiring, but it soon becomes a habit. You stop having to really think about it. You see the weed and react by pulling it, so your garden will always be beautiful. Not only that, but you can then spend time on other things because you don't have to focus on the garden so much. There are always little weeds here and there, but they don't override the beauty of the garden, nor do they get to hang around for a long time. If occasionally we feel the need to have a little break, it's okay because you can trust that there will always be a little voice to remind you gently that it's time to get back on track and pull the weeds. After you are refreshed, you will instinctively start pulling up weeds as they grow.

Visualize what those wonderful seeds will grow into in the future. What will you see, hear, and feel when you, like the seeds, are exactly where you want to be?

See the seed of the new you taking root in your future and begin to grow towards achieving everything you want. Perhaps you will have a sense of your next steps now, how you will move forward from here to greater and greater things. Perhaps you will see this time in your life as the start of something truly amazing for you.

Conclusion

The scene is now set for mindful eating to become part of your daily life forever. The following visualization will help you to reflect on your mindful eating journey and will spur you on to keep up your good work.

Imagine that we've laid the table with a crisp linen cloth, set out the finest silverware, and lit a beautiful candle centerpiece. The fresh, new ingredients are assembled, ready for you to prepare your perfect meal. As you sit down to savor your food, it's time to think about your mindful eating journey so far.

Perhaps you started with a feeling that mindful eating was accessible only to a select, spiritual few, or something to re-visit when you had more time on your hands. Yet now you are beginning to understand how it can work for you in your life, and how the simple principles of mindfulness can be applied to any everyday activity, without the need for an ashram or incense.

Your mindful eating goals are set and the light of awareness has been shone onto your eating habits; you know now that you can choose to change them and how you will go about doing so.

You know what constitutes a healthy, balanced way of eating, and how you can use this to become the best version of yourself. Food represents so much more than a collection of nutrients or calories, and you can use your new understanding to weave brightly colored variety throughout your life. You might have come across some pitfalls, limiting beliefs, or challenging emotions that were previously getting in your way, but you know how to deal with them mindfully from now on.

All you need to do now is keep practicing. The more you practice the better you become. Remember that just like learning to walk, every single step counts, no matter how small. So tuck in and enjoy your mindful meal now, one bite at a time. Savor and appreciate all the benefits that mindful eating has to offer you in your daily life.

Credits

RECIPES:

Ross Dobson

Three Sisters Soup; Spiced pumpkin, spelt, and goat's cheese salad; Spiced oatmeal cake with chocolate and cinnamon frosting; Spicy pinto bean soup with shredded lettuce; Slow-cooked lamb salad with beans, pomegranate, and fresh mint; Falafel with minted yogurt; Carrot and lentil dip

From *Cooking with Wholefoods* (Ryland Peters and Small, 2010)

Riverford Organic (www.riverford.co.uk)

Chorizo, chickpeas, lentils, and spring greens

Hazel Courteney and Nicola Graimes

Parchment-baked fish with herb dressing; Fig, almond, and raw cacao bars; Asparagus, chive, and pea shoot omelet; Herring with beets on sourdough rye; Roast cinnamon plums with pecan nuts

From *500 of the Healthiest Recipes and Tips You'll Ever Need* (CICO Books, 2012)

Rachel Anne Hill

Pan-fried salmon with white bean puree

From *500 of the Healthiest Recipes and Tips You'll Ever Need* (CICO Books, 2012)

Elsa Petersen-Schepelern

Fresh Virgin Mary; Italian lentil salad

From *500 of the Healthiest Recipes and Tips You'll Ever Need* (CICO Books, 2012)

REFERENCES

page 12 *Mindfulness: A Practical Guide to Finding Peace in a Frantic World* by Mark Williams and Danny Penman (Piatkus, 2011)

page 13 Research from the Mindfulness Report 2010, led by Dr. Andrew McCulloch

page 23 'Acres of Diamonds' story adapted from *Lead the Field* by Earl Nightingale (BN Publishing, 2007)

page 37 Adapted from *Sufis: The People of the Path* by Osho (Diamond Pocket Books, 2008)

Page 38 *The 7 Habits of Highly Effective People* by Stephen Covey (Simon and Schuster, 1989)

Page 78 *In Defence of Food: The Myth of Nutrition and the Pleasures of Eating* by Michael Pollan (Penguin, 2009)

Page 86 *The Blue Zones: Lessons for Living Longer from the People Who've Lived the Longest* by Dan Buettner (National Geographic, 2010)

Resources

USEFUL WEBSITES

The *TED: Ideas Worth Spreading* website (**www.ted.com**) contains many illuminating and inspiring videos on a range of diverse subjects.

For more information on Dan Buettner's work, **www.bluezones.com**

www.slowfood.com

www.riverford.co.uk for delicious, organic recipe ideas.

www.martinemoorby.com Martine offers grounded and practical training in EFT and Reiki at all levels.

BOOKS

In Defence of Food: The Myth of Nutrition and the Pleasures of Eating by Michael Pollan (Penguin, 2009)

The Blue Zones: Lessons for Living Longer from the People Who've Lived the Longest by Dan Buettner (National Geographic, 2010)

Living in the Moment by Anna Black (CICO Books, 2012)

Moro East by Samuel and Samantha Clark (Ebury, 2011)

The Happiness Project by Gretchen Rubin (HarperCollins, 2011)

Awareness by Anthony de Mello (Fount, 1997)

Transformational NLP by Cissi Williams (Watkins, 2012)

EFT for Weight Loss by Gary Craig (Energy Psychology Press, 2010)

Quiet the Mind by Matthew Johnstone (Robinson, 2012)

Index

Acknowledgments

We both owe particular thanks to all the participants on our mindful eating courses who have traveled with us on this special journey. Thank you for sharing your experiences with us and for all of your valuable feedback; we are both continually inspired by your amazing stories.

We are grateful also to the team at CICO Books who have provided us with this wonderful opportunity and given us encouragement, support, and great feedback along the way—in particular, Lauren Mulholland, Sally Powell, Louise Leffler, Jennifer Jahn, Elanor Clarke, and Meskerem Berhane. We also want to thank Amy Louise Evans for her beautiful illustrations.

Our sincere thanks goes to Ross Dobson, Hazel Courteney, Nicola Graimes, Rachel Anne Hill, Elsa Petersen-Schepelern, and Riverford Organic for sharing their delicious recipes with us. We would also like to thank Paul Fletcher; your help is much appreciated by us both.

Mandy would like to thank all her teachers and students of NLP, in particular Beryl Lyndley, Tina Kothari, Robert Dilts, and Judith Delozier who practice mindful NLP with heart. She would also like to give a particular shout out to the wonderful group of people at this year's Northern Reiki Retreat led by Martine Moorby who provided the perfect inspirational environment for her to write. Thanks also to Alison Wesson for proofreading the manuscript. Mandy would also like to give a special thank you to her wonderfully tolerant family for being there for her at the same time as dealing with A levels, GCSEs, and demanding jobs. And to Lizzie and Sam, and Max and Paddy, thanks for all the walks with pixies.

Rachel would like to thank all of her teachers and clients over the years for providing her with many opportunities to further her knowledge and understanding in this fascinating field. Thanks also to the wonderful team at Nutri Advanced Ltd who have been a great support for many years. Rachel would also like to thank her mum, dad, and two wonderful sisters for all their love and support over the years. Thanks also to Robert and Beryl for the extra help that gave me space to write. Rachel would like to give special thanks to her husband Jamie and her two children, Amelie and Tom, for always providing a home haven of love, support, encouragement, and inspiration. My thanks for all the treasured mountaintop picnics we've shared too; rain or shine, you're always there—thank you.